He Loves Me,
He Loves Me Not

He Loves Me, He Loves Me Not

Finding Homo Health & Happiness

Taylor St. Charles

Writer's Showcase
presented by *Writer's Digest*
San Jose New York Lincoln Shanghai

He Loves Me, He Loves Me Not
Finding Homo Health & Happiness

Writer's Showcase
presented by *Writer's Digest*
an imprint of iUniverse.com, Inc.

For information address:
iUniverse.com, Inc.
5220 S 16th, Ste. 200
Lincoln, NE 68512
www.iuniverse.com

Art & Design by Penelope E. Venola
Photography by Alexandra V. Smith-Ginter

ISBN: 0-595-12981-1

Printed in the United States of America

Contents

Foreword

The friendly couple next door haven't been in the neighborhood long, but they seem to fit in. That is as long as you don't expect to see them dancing at the Baptist Church social.

It turns out that, in the good old U.S. of A., currently over fifty percent of those sharing a home are not what was formerly your typical American family. In fact, in this case, your new neighbors are a male couple who just happen to be gay!

And, theirs is the home we'll visit. Not only that, Dorothy, we'll even take a peek into the bedroom!

To our heterosexual friends, I hope this is enlightening…maybe even interesting. To our lesbian friends, please excuse my references to exclusively male relationships. Frankly, I'm not adept as I might be in the lesbian scene. You have my admiration, and I would not presume to write things left better in your *very* able hands.

To lesbians, gays, bi's, and even to straights, I extend my hand in friendship and my arms in love. We all share this wonderful planet together, and understanding is the key to sharing it in peace.

I dedicate this informal thesis on gay friendships, and getting along in this mostly heterosexual world, to those wonderful people that make up the organization, Parents, Families and Friends of Lesbians and Gays (PFLAG), as well as to the memory of my loving father who would surely have been a member of PFLAG and who often copped out by saying, "Listen to your mother." And thanks Dad, I did.

As I was growing up I recall that Mother would jokingly say, "Would you buy a pair of shoes without trying them on? Then why would you marry a man before you'd slept with him?" Her name was Maryjane and she was a strikingly beautiful redhead. In her heyday she was rather like a dignified Tallula Bankhead. Maryjane married four times. Hopefully, at least one of them fit,…like a good shoe, that is!

In this book you'll find a bit of a "how to" guide; to avoid screwing up potentially wonderful relationships, as well as some tips on having a good time while making those relationships last.

I figure the greatest thing on earth is love. Second to love, and hopefully with it, come friendships. As I'm sure you know, friendships are varied; they can even include business/work relationships. And, oh yes, Mother would say: "Friendships should include your relatives, dear." But I'd be careful about that; we don't want to press our luck.

What does all this have to do with finding and keeping Mr. Right in the gay community? Well, let's just consider, there are really all kinds of us out there. (Yes, at least 10% of the world population belongs to our "club.") And yes, Dennis dear, there really is life after the bar scene. Let's accept the fact that most of us will live to be over 30 (gasp!) and someday, believe it or not, be willing to admit it.

You might call this a dissertation on how to get the most out of the gay scene…and how to make ourselves more desirable beyond the days of our youth…and even while we're still there.

Now don't get stage fright dearie! We won't go into the proper attire for aspiring to be crowned at the Empress Ball, or the right thing to say when participating in a "Mr. Gay America" contest. And heaven forbid that this should be meaningless dictations from some pseudo etiquette rules.

By the way though, I do agree with the definition of etiquette I found in *Cosmopolitan*: "…a combination of intuition, empathy, thoughtfulness, self confidence and poise." I'd say most of our gay community needn't worry about that last one, but I'm pretty sure we could all brush up on the other four. Of course Mother would remind me here to: "Speak for yourself dear!"

In addition to getting along and making ourselves appealing as friends, there is a philosophy I'd like to convey about gay liberation.

A thousand cheers for the brave men (including many in drag) who made history in June of 1969 as they rioted against New York's oppressive police at the Stonewall Inn…and applause too for all of those who still march with pride in our gay parades. But that's not the liberation to which I refer. In *How to be a Couple and Still be Free*, Riley Smith said: "Just as unmarried heterosexual couples, gays and lesbians also violate the traditional rules, so they must create new unprecedented concepts and methods of getting along." He suggested that we support one another, teach one another and, most important, that we love one another without unreasonable expectations. I believe that when we can do these things, then we have truly found our liberation.

Let's give this opportunity some serious thought. Okay, we've already bent the rules; how's about setting up some for our own good. This whole process of human relations will go smoothly only if we make thoughtfulness our rule of friendship. Like the "golden rule," we must never do unto others what we would not have them do unto us.

And now that we have liberated *that* closet door, let's begin thinking freely for *our own* good. After all the guilt we've had dumped on us as homosexuals, bisexuals, transsexuals or "straight, but willing to try," some may find it hard to open their minds to real self confidence and self respect. Okay, so there are those who disagree with our lifestyle, who disassociate themselves from us. If so, then they are the losers and it's good riddance without them.

*　　*　　*　　*　　*

First off I'd like you to invest some time to compile a list of *your own* good qualities. Do it! It's time well spent.

Perhaps you didn't graduate from a university. So you probably have a rugged individual, innocent (?), quality. That turns a lot of people on. Or maybe you wear glasses, you've always hit the books, and you've spent half of your adult life in college. Surprise! You are gorgeous to many and, to many, that college degree is a built-in father image. Okay, so you have a physical handicap, or maybe you're part of an ethnic minority (there are really very few left…maybe WASPs). Don't let a so-called handicap imprison you! Having overcome it, or having learned to live with it, has made you a very special person that many admire. And in the gay community admiration often translates into sex appeal. Believe it! We gays often criticize our own community as being too youth or good-looks oriented. Not so! (Well, maybe sometimes.) But we can also be the most broad minded, and we tend to have the most unusual trend setting talents and appeals, of any group around.

So take another look baby! You've got something special going for you…use it to your advantage! Stand straight (it helps if you suck in your gut); people will take notice, if they haven't already. Let yourself be the terrific person you really are!

I'm not saying to be an egotist. But give some self respect and loving care to that guy in the mirror, then you'll be pleased to know, others will give you special note as well.

While you're at it pal, let's spread that tender loving care around to others. As your Mother probably said, "You have to give in order to receive." You do know how to *give*, don't you?

1

Gay Lifestyle and You

What really makes our lifestyle "gay?" Just between us, I wish there was another word to describe it…queer or fag? Call me old fashioned, but no thank you. We've all heard the stories of how "gay" was a secret code word we used to describe ourselves in the thirties and forties. The French use "gai" which, like so many French words, seems to have a sophistication. I like that: "gai." It differentiates us from the frivolous English word that indicates an unreal state of pleasure. All right already! So I'll conform… at least this time, and we'll stick with "gay." At any rate our particular mind set, for what ever reason, has as its basis, the difference of having the homo- rather than hetero-sexual sources of attraction.

And, just like the heterosexual community, our major subconscious drive is, thank goodness, toward human bonding. Yah; sex is definitely a wonderful thing! Indeed the growth and security of our community is based on relationships with others of our own kind. It may be hard for some of us closet cases to admit, but most certainly, the underlying thing we have in common with other gays is our unique sexual orientation.

Much the same as the average heterosexual, an over-thirty active gay male is found to spend less than an hour in forty-eight involved in sex (or masturbation)…probably even less. So you're still in your youth? How about one in twenty-four? The remainder of his hours are spent doing much the same as his heterosexual counterpart. By the way, many experts in the field of sex therapy agree that a man reaches a sexual climax much faster than a woman. Where a woman requires 10 to 20 minutes to reach sexual arousal, a man can be aroused, have an erection and ejaculate in less than 3 minutes. It may also surprise many to learn that there are a large number of gays who, just as many straights (believe it or not) seldom indulge in sexual intercourse. Of course there are always those faithful five fingers. (Does that count?) Go ahead, who really cares? Well, maybe those conservative religious doctrines that preach antiquated "orthodox" restrictions that feed on sex being practiced to simply increase the population of their followers.

What I'm getting at is that the great preponderance of our gay *lifestyle* is more a way of thinking than it is a way of having sex.

So why make a big thing out of gay relations? For one thing, when the basis of one's subconscious drive is his or her attraction to others of the same sex, and a desire to share the creature comforts associated with "men only" (or women only) then you find parallel thinking on the part of friends…particularly other gays.

Do I play down the sexuality of gays? Yes. The reason? Even though sexual orientation is the basis of our being different from the majority (or norm, what ever that is) there is no more reason that a dissertation on gay human relationships should dwell on sex, than there is that a thesis on relationships among say, Indonesians, should dwell on their sexual patterns. Although that should be interesting! There is nothing to indicate that American gays spend any more of their waking hours having sex than do Indonesian straights.

So what is this about bars and other gay cruising places? Because, aside from the underlying themes, these are social gathering places and areas that make our community unique. And what goes on in these places? Communication! Sometimes it's only eye contact, sometimes it's hot pursuit. But more often than not, it's simply enjoying each other's companionship. And companionship is precisely why these relationships are important.

We're all on this planet for a relatively short period of time. None of us will come out of the experience alive! So why not make the best of it? At the local bar, the flashy disco, the sun swept beach, the professions we've chosen, brunch with friends, or a trip to Hawaii, baby, this is *your* life! And, what you get out of it depends solely on one person: *you*!

Mother often said, "We should be patient with others, as we hope they will be with us." And by the way, try sprinkling that patience with a good sense of humor. Laughter does wonders for the face…in addition to being good for your relationships, it's great for your health and well-being.

2

Enjoying Life

Psychologically our lives continue to be more and more complex. There is no question that the speed of our transportation, the immediate reporting of world catastrophes, the Internet, and the intricate computerized work place, have all created stressful conditions, whether we intend to accept them or not. And, of course, lesbians and gays (just as other minorities) have the added stress of always being on guard against bigotry.

Good heavens! What's a boy to do?

Well, right here and now, promise yourself that it's not going to get to you! Remember, this world we live in is *not perfect* (Mary Baker Eddy, the founder of Christian Science, said otherwise; but girl, it ain't so)...Nor are we, the people who reside here-on. So don't keep expecting perfection. Instead, look for the humor in things and accept people as they are. Remember also, that as much as you strive for perfection, you aren't perfect. Okay, so neither am I ! They thought Christ was perfect and he ended up nailed to a cross. The enlightenment of The Buddha came only after he accepted the world's imperfections.

If the work you do creates nothing but stress for you and you don't feel you are accomplishing your *personal* goals…take another look…is it really worth it? It's possible you're in the wrong profession. But if you're lucky, you enjoy your work and that's great! When you say your work is challenging, do you mean it's a stressful challenge, or do you enjoy accepting new opportunities that call for your kind of creativity? Then there are those that like to change their pace and their environment from time to time.

A Los Angeles Times article reported on a California State University at Long Beach professor who had done a research paper on "Fun in The Workplace." Shortly after that article came out, his work was also featured in *Forbes Magazine*.

In essence his conclusion was that those who are most successful, with the least amount of stress in their endeavors, are those who have fun at work. What is "fun" at work? First of all it is really enjoying what you do. It might be the kind of work that started as a hobby. Look at Bill Gates, the computer nerd who has become one of the richest men in the world. He wasn't looking to just make big bucks; he simply loved what he did.

Second, it's a pleasant environment. That includes the people with whom you come in contact on a regular basis. If the attitude at work is live-and-let-live, then you'll obviously not be up-tight. You don't let petty things get to you, you try and respond to challenges pleasantly and positively.   Some of the other reasons given for fun on the job are perks, such as going to lunch or dinner as a guest of the company, incentive trips and outings made available and paid for by the company. Probably more important than even financial return is the fact that those who consider themselves both happy and successful are those who feel comfortable in their profession. It is said that a man who is obviously enjoying his work will eventually be paid far more, in both money and good health, than the individual who is constantly striving for, but unable to attain, recognition and disproportionate remuneration. (Although I wouldn't turn down that sizable raise.)

I had an uncle who wrote about this philosophy. He called his book *The Third Commodity*. Uncle Al loved the restaurant business and he invented the sizzling steak process. At his Hollywood restaurant he established a friendship with several motion picture notables, and in his book he used several of them as examples: How even as a child Joan Crawford had been absorbed with the theater and how Walt Disney had always been enthralled with seeing children at play.

In a *Psychology Today* article by Curt Sandman, Ph.D., Dr. Sandman indicated that deliberately altering your activities with those that are different and ideally, fun, can create a mental atmosphere that actually improves ones memory. If you continue on with the same tedious, uninteresting job day after day, you may not only be in a rut, but it is far more likely that you will be forgetting details.

Psychology Today ran another article that was about coping with depression, written by Ann Rosenfeld, with conclusions drawn from studies by Doctors Susan Krantz, Rudolph Moos and James Coyne. In essence it said that, a person who has become so depressed that he is apathetic and withdrawn, and uninterested in most pleasurable activities (including, yes, even sex) may become so morose that he even considers suicide. This is a person who *must* have clinical help from an expert. It is also important that the patient's life-partner be counseled as well. A person who has gone through such a depressive episode could not help but create an atmosphere that negatively alters the environment and enjoyment of life in the home.

A University of Michigan study indicated that 40 percent of the spouses of those patients require treatment themselves. It also indicated that 17 percent of family unions were broken up as a result of these episodes. It is recommended that a life-partner have counseling in order to manage the stress created by a depressive episode. If you don't have a counselor to turn to, but you feel it may help, I suggest that you contact a Gay & Lesbian Community Center. They often have peer counselors, or they can refer you to a licensed therapist or psychologist.

If you or your partner have a reliance on drugs and/or alcohol, or there are religious or cultural pressures too overwhelming to handle, one should really seek help. On the other hand, if most conditions seem healthy and reasonable, you might just need some honest-to-goodness attitude adjustment. Don't be afraid to deliberately change the pace of your activities whenever possible. If economics require that you eat dinner at home most of the time, then take a healthy walk to a local bakery, an ice cream/yogurt shop or a coffee house for dessert. If you and your partner both work full time, go out to dinner a couple of nights a week…sometimes even separately for a break and a "breather." On the weekends go to places you haven't been for a while and simply "entertain yourselves." Don't be afraid to try something new. Just because you've never been to a ball game or an opera, don't be afraid to suggest it as something different. You just might get a big kick out of it simply because you know it isn't your usual beat. (Or something *really* different, like going in drag.) Have you ever been cruising? I mean on the water…in a big boat. Try a short one the first time to see how you like it.

Go to a technical exhibition in a field you may not have been interested in before. You may surprise yourself with a new interest. Have you ever been so tired Friday evening that you hit the sack early, only to find yourself wide awake at 4 or 5 AM on Saturday? Drive out into the country and watch the sun rise, then enjoy breakfast out there at your leisure.

Here's a way to enjoy getting ready for your next vacation: Once you've set the date and the destination, part of the pleasure comes from planning and anticipation. To enhance both the anticipation and the vacation, each time you have sex, agree to pay the "kitty" $2, $5 or even $10 each. Nothing that will break you, but enough to really build a fund. Then, when you're ready to blast-off (on the vacation, that is), you'll have the resources to enjoy those extra-special dinners at places you might otherwise have hesitated to splurge. What a way to keep life interesting…Paying yourselves for pleasure!

I know much of what I've suggested here about psychology relates to couples. If you're single, please don't let that stop you. As for the enjoyment of your career and your leisure, all of this applies, most importantly, to your own mental and psychological outlook on life. As for changing your pace and your activities; as a single person, it is that much easier to shift gears without having to be concerned about how it effects the other guy.

Enjoy this life to its fullest. The world may be billions of years old, but we're only here for a relatively short time. Make the best of it dear. And let's be honest with ourselves, except for a life-partner, in the final analysis, no one is going to give a damn about how much you got out of life but *you*.

3

Dealing with Prejudice

In the middle of the nineteenth century America grappled with its conscience. Would it continue to allow slavery and inequality, or would slavery be abolished, and would the states finally unite to become the great nation that our forefathers envisioned?

Abraham Lincoln reluctantly found himself at the center of a civil war, a war that would forever alter our nation's destiny. Because he had the courage and compassion to make the right decisions, there were many bigots who hated him and hated what he stood for. President Lincoln's abhorrent assassination brought grave sorrow to the overwhelming majority of Americans. Among those, was one of American's greatest poets, Walt Whitman.

It was at that time that Whitman was continuing to write his phenomenal composition, *Leaves of Grass*. He had first published the book in 1855, with only twelve poems. (Ultimately *Leaves of Grass* was comprised of 383 poems.) He was so deeply touched by Lincoln's assassination that in his book he created a lengthy commemorative: *Memories of President Lincoln*. In the tenth sonnet of that memorial he wrote:

"O how shall I warble myself for the dead one there I loved?
And how shall I deck my song for the large sweet soul that has gone?
And what shall my perfume be for the grave of him I love?
Sea-winds blown from the east and west,
Blown from the Eastern sea and blown from the Western sea,
      till there on the prairies meeting,
These and with these and the breath of my chant,
I'll perfume the grave of him I love."

Now, over a century later, we learn that both of these great and compassionate men had the inner love and the emotions of men that, in their day, was considered "the love that dared not speak its name." We know, of course, that Walt Whitman was one of America's most exalted authors. Yet, because of his views and his outspoken love for the martyred president, he was ridiculed by a few small minded and self-appointed critics of the day.

In addition to a multitude of other gays and lesbians throughout our history, America owes a tremendous debt of gratitude to the lives and the brilliance of both Lincoln and Whitman.

       *   *   *   *   *

On a lighter note, I recall my mother saying, we must avoid showing hatred. However, just between you and me, she couldn't help herself....She really *hated* paying taxes. And another thing she couldn't abide was people that implied they knew how she should live. Whenever I hear of those homophobes who try to tell us how *we* should live, I think of Mother's words of wisdom: "Honey, when they pay *my* taxes I *may* let them tell me how to live. And they needn't hold their breath, 'cause I'll *never* be paying theirs!"

The reverse of hate is love.

Centuries ago Confucius introduced a formalized creed encompassing the law of opposites, the universal balance of Yin and Yang.

Within each of us there are always these opposites. In order to deal with the extremes of our so-called civilization, war and peace, pain and comfort, hate and love, we must recognize the existence of these opposites.

Every twenty-four earth hours all living things are kept in balance by the brilliance and heat of the sun, then the quiet darkness and cool of night. In order to appreciate the full color spectrum we must view its wide variations. We can then appreciate the incredible range of colors between those extremes.

A person may cherish his own family one moment, then unfortunately he may turn to dislike or fear other humans simply because they are different.

In America, and indeed throughout the world, minorities are discriminated against, both socially and economically. Sometimes prejudice is blatant but, more often than not, it is quite subtle.

As homosexuals, what is it that makes us *different* from our friends and siblings? According to extensive research published by Doctors Alan P. Bell and Martin S. Weinberg in *A Study of Diversity Among Men and Women* (Simon & Schuster, 1978) "…homosexuality is not a definable entity but, rather, a *normal variation* of sexual behavior, erotic disposition, and sexual preference, expressed in varying degrees and manners by different individuals."

By society in general we have been placed in a category of being *different*, and therefore we are seen as a minority. It is tragic that bigotry continues to exist throughout the U.S. Here we are, a nation whose strengths come from our phenomenal diversity, we are made up of literally every race on earth. Yet, how sad it is that the African-America child must learn the curse of prejudice at an early age. Though in the United States we are all Americans by birth, those who may come from Hispanic, Asian, Jewish or various other ancestries, may be faced with the revolting menace of discrimination throughout their lives. Often parents, as well as peers, teach children to distrust and to fear those who don't look, think or act similar to themselves.

Then it comes as a shock to gays and lesbians in their teens, if not earlier, when they too must accept being different from their peers. Where the ethnic minority most often finds protection and support within the family, and within their ethnic community, the homosexual suddenly becomes aware that he or she is totally and very often desperately alone with this secret.

As a teenager or young adult, hopefully you have conquered your own inward prejudice against those who you see as "fags" or "dykes." But then, how did you cope with your personal and emotional hurt when those who were your pals made snide remarks about "queers" or "deviates," knowing those remarks might soon be directed at *you*?

Coming out to friends is not easy. You know it could cost you that friendship and, in the future, it could effect your social and even your business relationships. Every homosexual must weigh the pros and cons of how far to come out, and to whom. Coming out to members of your biological family can be a painful and emotional experience…not only for you, but also for your parents and siblings.

For those fortunate enough to have a well educated, understanding environment in the home, your own family is probably the place to start. (By well educated I don't just mean college degrees; Some of the most enlightened people I know are quite worldly, constantly soaking up knowledge and seeking out both old and new thought, yet they may have a limited formal education.)

Before coming out to either family or friends it is important to establish your own positive mind-set. Do not allow fear of the worst outcome to control your thinking. Have a personal "conference with yourself" to establish certain facts:

1. You did not choose to be homosexual and your parents did not establish this for you. Neither you nor your parents (or any other person) had anything to do with your sexual orientation.

2. Being homosexual is no more the outcome of your parents or environment than is the fact that you may happen to be right or left handed. According to extensive scientific research, you cannot blame or thank anyone for your sexual orientation.

3. Because you *did not* have a choice, your sexual orientation can not, by anyone's standard, be considered morally wrong. So-called religious directives that may teach otherwise are not based on love; those negative interpretations (and they *are* simply interpretations) are based on ignorance and bigotry.

4. Be proud of yourself as a worthwhile human being. You have a great deal to offer the world. Remember, historically, the thousands of great minds, the teachers, the leaders and artists, who have been and are homosexual or bisexual.

5. Be considerate of the ignorant who fear homosexuality …they may be uncertain of their own sexual orientation. Remember that ignorance and fear are usually the cause of bigotry. *But bigotry can be cured!* (I know, because as a child I harbored racial bigotry.)

6. The family member or friend to whom you may divulge your homosexuality may find it hard to understand at first. Allow him or her some time to absorb this surprise before going into very much detail. (Remember how long it took *you* to accept *your own* sexual orientation.)

7. And lastly, make the positive assumption, and *convey this assumption*, that your confidante is kind and open minded.

Gradually, after coming out, you may find your family relationships and your circle of friends may change and expand. You will probably have some very pleasant surprises the way certain members of your family respond, making your love for them even stronger. If you are as fortunate as I was, they'll let you know that they enjoy knowing that other part of you, and that there will be a stronger bond between you.

On the other hand, even with your positive mind-set, if some members of the family or long-time friends are still fearful and seem unable to accept this reality, you will find fellowship in a huge worldwide gay community. Indeed, the gay community exists in every section of the world and at every social and business level. In addition, there is another level of friends, who may be bi or hetero. They're friends that know your orientation and are quite comfortable with your lifestyle. My youngest niece and her husband are typical. I didn't want to say they were "fag hags," and they were more than simply "gay friendly," so I asked if my niece could come up with an appropriate term?

She thought for a while, then said, "Let me get back to you on that one." A couple of weeks later, I had nearly forgotten my question, when out of the blue she called me and said: "I found it! Now don't box me in, Unc, but I'd like to think of myself as "homosocial."

Terrific! *Homosocial* it is!

I sympathize with every ethnic person who finds himself in a strange environment. But lesbi-gays take heart! From extensive travels throughout the world (including some most enjoyable research) I am delighted to report that *we are everywhere*…10% of the world population is a very conservative estimate. Plus, we have our good friends, the *homosocials*.

What I am saying to you who may feel alone is: It is not difficult to find your gay brothers and sisters anywhere on earth. Naturally you will want to be discrete and, of course, be very careful in unfamiliar areas for your personal safety. But if you want to seek out new friends, you literally have a world of opportunity.

Remember if you can that bigots are to be pitied and, if necessary, avoided. There are so many good people in the world; don't let those who are not, bring you down to their level.

Along this line, in doing research into current modes of conduct, I am pleased to report that it's considered improper for people to make embarrassing inquiries into one's sexual orientation. As one heterosexual expert on etiquette put it: "A hostess was asked if her friends were homosexual and she answered, 'I don't know; I wouldn't *dream* of asking them such a personal question!'" Furthermore, if a host or hostess feels some straights appear to be uncomfortable about a couple of gay or lesbian friends being invited to one's party, it is the problem of those who are uncomfortable, not the problem of the hostess or the gays.

Through experience we might learn how to answer those whose questions are too personal and/or whose motives are questionable.

I recently saw an interview on TV of a very successful composer/ entertainer. After considerable discussion about his many hit songs, the host asked this middle aged Hispanic if he had a family, and did his career and travels bring about any conflict with his family life. The entertainer answered "yes," and went on to tell how close he was to his parents and his sisters. Then he smiled and said he wasn't married, and had no children that he knew of. The TV host chuckled, and the uncomfortable question became something of a joke.

During most of my adult life I've been in either the hotel or travel business. I find the most concern that lesbians and gays have in traveling is how to ask for accommodations for two people of the same sex.

Look at it this way. Millions of people of the same sex share accommodations when traveling on business. And some share during vacations simply because its economical.

You don't need to make a big deal out of sharing. When you arrive at a hotel, don't go in thinking they're assuming things and they're homophobic. First off I can bet you that the majority of those on the front desk are either gay or homosocial. Say that you're making your reservation, or checking in at a hotel and you really want one king or queen size bed. Simply say so. If that twerp at the desk gives you any flack, ask for the front office manager or resident manager, then clarify your request. Remember, you're the guest and it's your money. If you don't have a non-refundable deposit and they aren't cooperating, make it a point to tell them you have a choice, and use another hotel.

In business dealings, another way I have found to deal with prejudice is through the art of psychological Judo. In Judo one uses the attack of the opponent to win against his confrontation. If I find myself having to deal with a person who is obviously hateful, I try very hard *not* to show my dislike for the individual. As they say in cards, "Don't show your hand." However, over a matter of time, if I must continue to deal with this individual, I allow him or her to "dig his own grave." By not allowing this individual the pleasure of getting the best of me, I ultimately find that I have the opportunity to make decisions that may favorably or adversely effect him or her without that person being aware of the source of the outcome. As the John F. Kennedy family use to say: "Don't get mad, get even." Or, better yet, as you prosper remember that "living well is the best revenge."

Yes, unfortunately, ignorant bigotry does exist. We can consider the source or, if necessary, deal with it on *our own* terms.

On a recent RSVP vacation, each evening my partner and I found a printed note along with a *good night mint* on our my pillows. One of the messages went something like this: "The next time someone asks you, 'Hey, howdja get to be a homosexual anyway?' Tell them, 'Homosexuals are chosen first on talent, then interview, then the swimsuit and evening gown competition pretty much eliminates the others.'" By the way, for me, enjoying an RSVP cruise is the *sweetest* revenge.

4

Cool Cruising

Wherever you cruise, be it in the bars, on the beaches, in the baths (now better known as health clubs), at private parties or, ah yes…by ship, bad manners and tackiness may get you momentary notoriety, but they won't get you Mr. Wonderful.

You may say, "aren't good manners old fashioned?" If you think so, consider the tactless "bitches" you've observed. Would you trade places with them? Who can get along without good manners? Possibly the very wealthy or very virile and handsome. But no one sincerely cares for a wealthy jerk or a self-centered egotist. Ignorance and age will one day steal away their precious wealth and/or good looks.

My partner and I were enjoying breakfast at a restaurant in San Francisco. Nearby were three lovely male locals. I should say, two were lovely, one was a bitch. In a loud, obnoxious voice, this one was giving the waitress a hard time. Among other things, he found fault with the coffee. The waitress, who was being as courteous as possible, took away the offending cup of coffee. And in a short while a *waiter* appeared with a fresh cup. The bitchy one said there was another problem, and he wanted to talk to the *waitress*. The new waiter asked what was the problem. Well, he only wanted to speak to the *waitress*. The waiter said the waitress was on her break and that he would be serving them. Well!

This waiter knew how, in a very subtle but a most *superior* way, to verbally out bitch the old queen. You get the picture? It was a show we wouldn't have missed for anything!

While we're feeling terribly smug about *our* good manners and tactfulness, let's not forget the values of compassion, warmth and sincerity. Yes dear, be sincere!…whether you mean it or not.

So you are self-confident, in touch with reality, handsome in your special way and you want to communicate with another of like interests (and hopefully looks that appeal to you). Well, Mother often said, "It takes two to tango, and unless you're in step with your partner, you'll both fall on your posteriors." (Her way of saying *asses*.)

Verbally the way to be in step with Mr. Right is not to bruise his ego. (Unless it's kiddingly, after you have become *very* good friends.)

The difference between a tactful statement and a cutting jab that pierces the ego is quite subtle. If you want to make friends and influence certain people, you must get used to knowing the difference. Here are some do's and don'ts:

1. He's thirty-five and admits he's never had a lasting relationship. Don't:

   "Oh really; you've lived alone all these years?" Do: "It must be nice to be so free—to come and go as you please."

2. He tells you he's made reservations for a vacation in Mexico this summer. Don't:

   "Mexico's weather is too damn hot and humid in the summer." Do: "What a terrific vacation. If I could get away, I'd beg to be a stow-away."

3. The hunk sitting next to you on the plane is obviously nervous, and says he hates to fly. (He's scared shitless.) Don't: (While

wishing you could hold his wet hand) "But jets seldom have accidents—except on take-off and landing." Do: "Are you flying to Miami on business or pleasure?" Get him started to thinking about something other than the plane and accident statistics.

4. Your friend at work is late and the boss knows—in fact the boss is pissed-off about it. Don't: "The boss was in, he's pissed, and he's looking for you!" Do: Leave a note that Mr. Jones wants to see him. (He's saving face with you and you haven't put him on the spot.)

5. Your friend has failed at a work or sports endeavor and he's feeling low. Don't: You couldn't help it; why don't you just forget it." Do: "Okay, so you can't win them all. You'll make it big the next time around. (You understand him, and he learns from his mistakes.)

6. He suggests a microwave dinner and video at your place or his. But you aren't ready for that much closeness yet. Don't: "Let's not stay in. I'm not up to video tonight." Do: I think it would be less of a strain on my willpower if we went out this time."

And, for matters of life or death...

7. You're out with a friend. He has his car, but he's become intoxicated. Don't: "You're too bombed to drive your car, let alone, find it!" Do: "I love your Jaguar; Could I drive us home?" If that doesn't work, and he's out of it, just demand the keys or insist on a cab. He probably won't remember it the next day anyway.

8. You'd love to get in bed with him, but he's had too much to drink and/or you don't trust the ability of either of you keeping it to safe-sex. Remember, with good judgment you'll both enjoy this for many years to come. A lack of safe-sex control is simply suicide. Don't: "Stop that, I'm just not interested!" Do: "I like you very much and I am interested, but I think we'll have to give this more time." If he can't handle that, or doesn't want to wait, maybe this is the time to clear up this relationship.

These may all sound a bit trite and stiff. You may be way past the "handle with care" stage. Then just consider using these suggestions as general guidelines. The most important thing to remember in human relationships, whether with your boss, co-workers, family or friends—everyone has an ego, so do handle with care and compassion.

Oscar Wilde once said: "A gentleman is one who never hurts anyone's feelings…unintentionally." And what a "mother" she was!

5

Compatible Groups

Before AIDs there was a subconscious envy among many of our heterosexual friends because of our ability to enjoy what seemed like unlimited sexual freedom. The epidemic certainly changed all of that! But something that has actually improved is the huge number of special interest groups where one can socialize in the gay community.

At last count there were over 300 gay organizations in the Los Angeles area alone. And, according to a national task force, there are well over 2,000 gay and lesbian organizations in the United States. Of course I'm not one to brag, but Mother said, "If you don't blow your own horn, no one's going to blow it for you."

While Goodie-twoshoes is moping about in his apartment, saying: "Why can't I find my dreamboat?" He seems blind to the thousands of special interest groups, having dancing lessons, rap sessions and going camping...like in the woods.

If you're gay dear, there just isn't any reason to be lonely. Unless, of course, you're into self pity. (Now aren't *we* being the bitchy one.) And how do you find these fun groups? Well, for starters, just look in a telephone directory under Gay. Yes, you'll usually find a Gay and Lesbian Community Center in any large city. Call and ask if they can direct you to a group with your particular interests, like religious, political, hobby, sports, or the professions. If you can't find a community center in your area and you have a little nerve, contact your nearest university or political volunteer group. On college campuses you'll usually find a gay students association or support group.

By the way, once you've found Mr. Wonderful, there's an international gay couples organization. What's more, for later years, there are now well established gay seniors support groups in many major cities.

6

Making Friends

In gay life there are two kinds of close friends. The first, rare and very unique, are those with whom you fall in love. The second, are those extra special people who are simply close personal friends or "best friends." We once called them "sisters," but fortunately the femme vernacular is no longer popular.

Let's go with the second category first...the first is a whole different line of thinking, courting, sharing and, of course, loving. (More on that later.)

Several years ago I shared a Caribbean cruise with one of those special best friends. Off and on all week we touched on memories of college days, being drafted into the army, sharing our overseas experiences, even, believe-it-or-not, marriages to women, child rearing and now, new opportunities and responsibilities as single gay adults.

We both agreed that it's a terrific feeling knowing there is someone out there who really understands. We both know the crazy and unusual way we look at things. Here's a friend who is always willing to listen and to be a sounding board about frustrations, career endeavors, joys, exciting experiences and, of course, gay encounters.

We both know, as much as we think alike, on some subjects we may think quite differently. This friend simply personifies that wonderful experience I consider more gratifying than any material or ego building career achievement. It's the experience of knowing we share our lives with those beautiful, crazy, predictable, and often unpredictable people we call our best friends.

I'm not promoting the development of cliques or exclusive groups. But I am promoting the giving of our time, energy, consideration and love in the building of friendships. The returns are more valuable than any material wealth.

I have enjoyed many examples along this line since my hetero-marriage break-up. For instance, the first few months when I was living alone, along came Thanksgiving. I had asked my ex-wife and our son out to dinner. But I had also met a couple of gay men who I figured hadn't been invited to Thanksgiving dinner. So I invited them to my apartment for brunch. They both accepted, and we had a most enjoyable day.

A few years later my new partner and I had planned a trip to San Francisco for Thanksgiving. One of the two that had come to brunch had become a close friend of ours. He and a friend of his invited us for Thanksgiving dinner. Because of the trip we couldn't accept. But we both felt a warm appreciation for their thoughtfulness. Had we been in town, we would have certainly welcomed the opportunity.

Of course this isn't an unusual situation. But the point is, we create our own karma. We all have hundreds of opportunities, in many ways, to be kind to others and to create friendships. But these friendships don't just happen. We have to make the effort.

*   *   *   *   *

Mother would say, "You must accept your friends for what they are, not what you want them to be." Of course, if you can't stand some clod, ignore him. The friendships you build are of your own doing…go for it!

Do you enjoy being alone? Simply devoting time to meditation, to music, hobbies or book reading? That's great! I have immense respect for the self-dependent.…even a reclusive life-style has precious value. If that's the life you prefer, then the first rule is to know yourself and appreciate yourself. I strongly recommend a thorough self analysis and understanding of self worth before attempting encounters with the outside world. Others can sense when you are happy with your own being…at peace with yourself. I have a few friends who never intend to pair up with a steady lover or partner. They get along very well alone, and as well with friends. In addition to encounters now and then, these men have interests in their careers and many other activities. They really have their feet on firm ground. They have a good philosophical outlook interwoven with a healthy self esteem.

And I know of many gays and straights who have high regard for these men as good businessmen and as personal friends.

However, if the single life isn't your cup-of-tea, don't knock it. To each his own…and for the rest of us, let's talk about making friends.

First off, there's nothing wrong with getting to know people in the bars. Bars are simply different spaces with different names. Just because you hit the bars doesn't mean you have to over indulge on booze. In fact, you will probably be a better conversationalist if you can keep your mind clear for the obvious pursuits. And very few people, except possibly the bartender, will notice if you just order sparkling water or 7-Up with a wedge of lime. Believe me, the bartender will be just as pleased that his tip comes from a sober person. What's more, if all goes well, it will be a delight getting acquainted with a new friend who won't feel that he's the target of aggression by some semi-drunk. Then, as a sober driver, when you get to "your place or mine," it will be great to have a clear head.

Of course, other than bars, there are hundreds of ways to meet other gays if we put our minds to it. First off, I believe gays really do have a second sense of knowing who is and who isn't. It's known as "gaydar" (gay radar). Personally I wouldn't rely on gaydar 100%...as we used to say, "it's best to keep one's hairpins in place 'til you know for sure." Even at work you may find many opportunities to get to know people in-depth and beyond the usual career level.

All right, so that could take forever, and maybe you don't want to risk exposure for fear that it could threaten advancement and raises. Anyway, keep your mind and eyes open for the possibilities. If you're in a major metropolitan area there are sure to be organizations such as the Great Outdoors, or the Metropolitan Community Church or other gay religious groups. If not, don't hesitate to phone a church such as Methodist or Episcopalian, a synagogue or a temple (have I left any out?). You needn't give your right name on the phone. Just ask if they have a gay outreach program. Of course, if you need to be closeted, don't ask your own church unless you know someone there well enough. I find that the Universalist Unitarians are very receptive to all lifestyles, but be prepared that their interests seem often more political than religious. And that's okay too.

You might also consider volunteering for some political activities. Usually the more liberal groups include, or at least accept, gays. By the way, if you have to write to a gay community center asking for information, don't forget to enclose a stamped self addressed envelope. If you are new to the gay scene, you may be pleased to learn there are gay organizations with interests as varied as there are politics, hobbies and careers. Here are a few: Doctors, scientists, alcoholics support, parents & friends, divorced, various professions, camping, couples, athletics, ethnic racial backgrounds, teachers, study groups, HIV and AIDs support, plus many more. Usually you aren't required to be from that particular interest or background, as long as you have a sincere interest in the topics at hand. For instance, Asian Pacific Gays and Friends welcome others who are simply interested in those cultures and peoples.

Some public places that are worthwhile for meeting people are museums, especially the specialized ones where you have an opportunity to exchange comments with those who may look interesting. Also swap meets and libraries present opportunities to enter into conversations and exchange ideas. Large furniture stores, antique shops and art stores, florists and travel agencies present opportunities to get to know the sales people and sometimes others in the store.

As for public rest rooms (also known as "tea rooms"), I don't recommend them due to individuals that become over enthusiastic and, of course, there is the vice squad. If you must make contact there, the only contact should be a knowing glance and "hello." Any additional conversation or action is out of the question…wait until you're way outside and away from the facilities. But even there, just as in any public place, be extremely careful of vice cops, hustlers and especially gay bashers.

When participating in gay organizations, here are a few guidelines that can also apply with straight organizations. If you are really interested in the subject matter and the people, attend on a regular basis. Be willing to help—in fact volunteer—when needed. If you'd like to become an officer, remember to speak out in a positive way. Notice the people in the group who put in extra effort and are leaders. Remember to tell them that you admire what they are doing. This is a very important part of group politics and the building of friendships. Remember, it's always nice to be appreciated. On the other hand, if you find someone in a group, or in your business, that for some reason seems to be detrimental to you, be sure to be *extra nice* to that person. It is very difficult for a person to cut you down when you have been particularly nice to him or her. You don't have to be gushy…that becomes obvious.

If you find yourself involved in a group meeting, make constructive comments and avoid arguing. No one wants to be associated with a

chronic complainer. If you find someone in the group that really interests you, and he too is enthused about the organization's subject matter,
you can take one of two positions. (Doesn't that sound familiar?) If he's
a strong dominant type (oh boy!) you can offer to help and maybe
encourage him to run for an office in the group. Or, if he seems to enjoy
looking up to you, let it be known that you would like to become more
involved—attend board meetings if they are open to members—and
offer to help on a committee, then run for an office yourself. Of course,
avoid running against Mr. Wonderful in case you may have more interesting ideas for him. Another thing: if someone else is obviously better
qualified, and has possibly been involved longer than you have, consider
offering your support and encourage others to give him or her their
votes. He or she will remember the next time around, and you'll have a
ready made constituency. (He owes you one.)

With all of this though, remember, this is only a group of friends. Try
to keep it that way. If politics get hot, heavy and nasty, don't let your ego
get the best of you. You could lose some very nice friends and end up
wishing you hadn't volunteered. If the situation seems to be heading
toward the sticky and unpleasant, it's best that you back off and simply
enjoy being a supportive member. If you play your cards right, you'll
meet many nice friends, maybe some day be president or chairperson if
you like, then turn over the reins to others, and your leadership will
remain a pleasant memory for all.

This is not to say that participating in a gay organization is all
peaches and cream…it can have some negative sides. If you don't want
personal publicity and you need, for what ever reason, to keep that
closet door closed—then best you let this be known to the officers and
simply enjoy participation and support on the side lines. You should
always be aware that involvement in a gay organization can be detrimental to others as well. Be considerate of the privacy and careers of
others in the group. Don't call a fellow member's home and leave a message with a relative that you don't personally know, that he is needed to

help out at the Gay Festival. The same goes for consideration of his job. Don't bring along an obviously swishy friend that may, unknowingly, create a scene. Or when Mr. Jones' secretary asks if you have an appointment, be business-like, even if you'd like to be otherwise when you know Mr. Jones slept with your lover the night before.

If you want to "out" someone, do it to a real enemy, not to another gay that is otherwise your ally. We simply must support those around us and use the same code of behavior that is expected from straights, whether in the business community or in the privacy of a family environment.

Now that you've had many opportunities to meet new gay friends, how do you go about establishing a special rapport; that certain something that helps the other guy remember you pleasantly at your next meeting? How do you make yourself a desirable person to have around...to be asked over for that party, brunch or pot luck?

I have a philosophy I call "mirrored personalities." When ever you find yourself at a loss for words (it has always happened to me when I have finally had an opportunity to talk with Mr. Right) just remember the mirror...your personality should reflect those good and attractive things from the other person, *don't* try to outshine him.

Start with any subject you like. It can be as simple as noticing his tennis shoes. "Do you jog?" Or, "Do you like the xyz brand of shoes for any particular kind of sport?" He may say "Yes, I like to wear them to bed." His response may be a pleasant surprise. And if he has a good sense of humor, you may eliminate a lot of superfluous chit-chat. When you are curious or complimentary about him, he can't help but realize that you are a friendly person and that you just might be interested.

Should there be a lull in the conversation, *and he hasn't run away*, go ahead and ask other things about him. Frankly, we all like to talk about ourselves. You don't go around looking for someone who will talk about you. But if someone happens to start talking about your favorite subject, it's hard to tear yourself away. Right? Now while you have his attention, seek out his opinions. Most people like to tell you what they think, but prefer not to have a disagreement. You don't have to give him your views, if they aren't compatible with his. But if you agree, then you've found levels of mutual interest. Or, maybe you find he is an intellectual who enjoys comparing various opinions on a subject. That is stimulating and makes for an expansion of your mental abilities. Just remember that fortunately, we aren't all alike; if we were it would be a pretty boring world.

Granted, most people don't like a perfect stranger to get too nosy...especially on the first meeting. But if you really listen to his responses and show that you are interested, you'll have an opportunity to learn something about him. This little *interview* will be an opportunity for you to learn if you really want to pursue this guy any further. Or possibly you'll learn that you have so little in common that you'd prefer to go on to greener pastures. Then be nice. Tell him you've enjoyed meeting him, and possibly you'll see each other another time.

You haven't committed yourself to anything. You're not going to bed with him. You aren't enemies. Remember him, he may have some very nice friends.

Then there are those we meet who tend to put themselves down. We've all found the same kind in the straight community. Personally I don't relate easily to that kind of individual. Perhaps he likes to play the subservient who enjoys being the "slave." Maybe you're the type that likes being the "master." To each his own. But, my dear, I think you'll find that your "slave" has deeper problems that will worsen in the years to come. Don't let me stop you, *Sir!* I'm sure I won't.

Back to the mirror. If you find this process works for you...that you have made it a habit to really get interested in the other person, then take mental notes. In fact, if necessary, actual notes (not in front of him, as if you were writing a book) if he's really responding and there's that exchange of names and phone numbers. Ah yes, we use to call them "trick cards." Anyway, this is the beginning of your personal file. My Dad called it his little black book. (Maybe it ran in the family.) But it's what you do with those cards that's important. In the past, maybe 80% of them went into the circular file. Then I suggest you re-think your system.

If you really want to develop friendships, follow up with a call the next day. So he may not be that interested, but it's worth a try. If you were smart, you noted some of his special interests and/or statistics after your meeting. Let him know that you enjoyed meeting, then mention something of interest to him. Keep up that "mirror," and without being gushy remember to reflect on his good points. If you'd like to meet again, even if only as friends, suggest he might participate in some outing or function that may be of interest to him. Or, don't hesitate to ask if he'd like to join you and a few friends for a "pot luck" next Sunday. People really feel comfortable with a person who allows them to participate and bring a part of the meal. It's not being cheap, it's simply letting a person join in on an equal basis.

About those "trick cards." Get a small filing box, or just start with a rubber band. Buy some 8X10 cards, set them up alphabetically…Or, just a rolodex. This way you can keep track of your friends' names, addresses, phone numbers, likes, interests, birth dates, etc. Of course there will be drop-outs; those whose interests really don't mesh with yours. There will be those who move away and, after a few holiday cards, you may loose touch. But those with whom you stay in touch will be a very valuable group to you, and may someday be considered your extended family…or even better!

Speaking of attention to friends: Have you ever been involved in a conversation with someone and suddenly realized you might as well be talking to a wall? Crazy? No, you just met someone who is probably a social climber. You know the type. Some of the so-called best politicians are guilty of standing in front of you as if giving you their full attention, but actually looking right past you. Either he's cruising or he's just spotted a hot political donor and, for either reason, is trying to get his or her attention.

I'm sure we've all had this happen (not necessarily from a politician) at some time. Or perhaps we've been guilty of it ourselves. The point is, if you have established contact with someone who is giving you his attention, don't be rude! Look at your friend and give him your full attention. So you see another friend come into the room or area. Allow the topic of conversation to end, then do the really wonderful thing and introduce the person you're talking with to Mr. Wonderful. Seriously, you certainly have ample self-confidence and poise to do the courteous thing:

1. Pay full attention to the one who is speaking;
2. Look him in the eyes;
3. Bring people together with introductions.

While on introductions, if you don't have a photographic mind (like 99% of us) you may forget someone's name. To avoid forgetting, make a real effort to repeat his name when you first meet. Everyone likes to hear his name. If you can associate his name, in your mind, with something or someone, make a mental note of it.

But if like mine, your memory tends to get lazy, then admit it and poke fun at yourself for not remembering. That's hard to do isn't it? Well, give it a try anyway. Your friends will consider you an honest pal if you level with them. Your lack of memory isn't as important as you may think. But they'll certainly remember that friendly, gregarious, guy that obviously made it a point to break the ice and helped people to get to know one another.

Here's another item you may want to jot down in your friendly memory: Avoid chewing gum or smoking while talking. Really, chewing gum while talking looks gross! And, if you smoke, take into consideration those with you who crave clean air. I understand…So you've got to have a cigarette to feel comfortable. Then, make it a point to clearly and sincerely state that you can hold off if it bothers your friends. Look and listen to the reaction to your offer. If there is *any* indication that it may bother someone, excuse yourself for a few moments and take a drag in the rest room or outside. If others agree, really agree, that it's okay with them, then place the ash tray where the smoke won't go their way. When exhaling smoke, make it a point to face away from the others. You may think I'm too fussy about this. But, believe me, there are those who simply must avoid the company of smokers…especially smokers who are inconsiderate of others around them. Consideration in this, just as in so many other relationships, is a very key factor in making and keeping good friends. If you don't care for the friendship of those who feel this way about cigarette smoke, maybe you'll need to limit your friendships to those who smoke.

7

Keeping Friends

Mother always said: "Good manners shouldn't be stilted; they should be friendly and sincere."

Those who have been considered great leaders have been those with compassion and courtesy. Our compassion is shown in our ability to get along with others. Basically you'll find that those who have reflected the quality of good manners have been those who are historically and most favorably remembered.

In recent history John F. Kennedy, Martin Luther King and Doug Hammershold were all known for their sincere courtesy…each had a gracious ability to put common workers, statesmen and heads of state at ease. A constant international party host, Frederick The Great, was known to always send written invitations to his soirees…he didn't want his guests to think he took them for granted. Even "rough and ready" Teddy Roosevelt took pleasure in the advance reading of subjects that were of interest to his guests. It is with such considerations that thoughtfulness becomes a complimentary footnote to the biographies of the famous.

Some are envied for their wealth and possessions. But those who, long after material wealth has vanished, retain the valued love and friendship of their fellow men, are those with good manners…a reflection of their respect and empathy for others. As long as we keep in mind our consideration for, and interest in, our friends and associates, they will naturally enjoy our company, and retaining their friendships will come quite naturally.

Are you honest to the core, or are you tactful?

Mother always said, "Better that you make up a nice lie someone wants to hear, rather than be brutally honest."

Have you ever been invited to dinner, to find that your host bought take-out food, then burnt it when re-heating? It happened to my partner and me.

We endured the burnt food without comment. Then afterward I was grateful we had held back our remarks. We came to find out that he was having a terrible personal problem that we weren't aware of at the time. Far more important than any smart-ass comments about the food, was our much needed companionship at that time in his life. Now that it worked for me, I feel it's wise to give this advise: Find something pleasant to say…don't be a complainer if you're someone's guest. Talk about the great wine, the background music, that blue shirt that goes with his eyes…anything! But don't be mean.

Finally you've received an invitation to visit your lover's parents. The house turns out to be tacky beyond belief! How could such a nice man, with such good taste (he picked you, didn't he?) have come from this?! Well, later, if the subject comes up, first mention that his folks were really nice…and that their place made you feel right at home. You've made your lover feel good, and you've reinforced the fact that their son chose a compassionate and tactful partner. Forget what your lover might think of your taste. He knows your choices only too well.

Remember, no one really wants to hear bad reports or negative comments. They get enough of that in the daily news.

8

Entertaing &
Being Entertatined

Want to feel confident when laying out the table? Take a look at the basic table setting: the knife, fork and spoon. The fork goes on the left, knife and spoon to the right. Always face the cutting edge of a knife inward.

With silver, remember that each fork, knife and spoon is placed outward from the plate with the utensil for the first course on the outer side. In other words, in addition to the main course, a salad might come first, so place a salad fork on the outer side to the left. If serving a soup, then the soup spoon goes to the outer right side.

Again, the outside utensils are intended to be used first...the ones closest to the plate will be used last. Fancy dessert spoons or forks are placed cross-wise, centered, above the setting. (See the *Formal Setting.*)

As a guest, this could all become confusing, right? If you're baffled, allow a host or hostess to begin eating first. Then you can play it safe by following his or her example. If he or she isn't at the table when it is obviously time to start, then follow the lead of the eldest. By the way, even if the host uses what you think might be the wrong utensil, it's safer to just follow his lead because he probably set the table. Otherwise you may end up minus the utensil you need for a course. Avoid being correct to the embarrassment of your host. Good manners are not a game of one-upsmanship.

China and glassware are generally placed in a fairly standard arrangement. The amount of table space and style will dictate how far outward each table setting can extend. If space permits, a place setting for seafood or fruit cocktail, bread & butter, entree with vegetable, potato or rice, and water goblet, could extend fairly far, like the *Celebration Setting*.

The easiest placement for the napkin is folded, at the left of the fork, or forks, or, if there's a salad plate, to the left of that. When placing a simple folded napkin to the left, the openings of the napkin should be at its lower left corner. (See the *Basic Setting*.)

This makes it easy for your guests to open the napkin with their left hand, not having to search for the openings. It's also fun to get fancy with your napkins, folded like flowers, tents, birds, etc. If you do that, you can show them off by placing them on your elegant (or understated) service plates at the beginning of the meal. Anyone for origami? Another fun thing, especially if you don't happen to have flowers on the table, is to let napkins "bloom" out of wine goblets. (You've probably seen it done in restaurants.) It all depends on what kind of show you want to put on for dinner.

By the way, while we're putting on these entertaining "shows," or any other time for that matter, avoid snobbishness or pretension. Those who look down their noses at others are those who are least apt to be trusted as friends. When you have guests over, it's definitely the thought that counts. Do as you please, but *don't* get yourself all exasperated with the minute details of setting the table (now he tells me!) or become exhausted with extensive preparation of fancy and elaborate dishes.

- *Table Settings* -

Celebration Setting

Formal Setting

Basic Setting

Napkin Decor

Okay, I can hear you saying: "So what the hell does setting a table have to do with finding *Mr. Wonderful?*" Well, my excuse is that, now or later, you're going to find yourself in the mood to entertain and I'm hoping that these tidbits might not only be a good reference, but they'll help you feel self confident while entertaining your special friend(s).

At any rate, when the time comes that you're up to inviting guests over, I'm sure the food will be palatable and the place will be fairly neat. After all is said and done, just remember that your friends aren't there for a food show, although gourmet cooking is obviously appreciated; they've come to see you and enjoy your company. Ralph Waldo Emerson had a knack for saying things just right: "The ornament of a house is the friends who frequent it."

Often the wealthiest and, even more important, the most interesting people, care very little if at all about being pretentious. As a matter of fact, if you *overdo it*, your guests might even feel a bit uncomfortable.

Now back to the food service: You can start with the salad already served, setting it on a service plate (optional), making it the center of each place setting. Then after the salad is eaten, remove the salad plate and, if included in your menu, place the cup of soup on the service plate. The service plate should be removed before the entree. If space requires, or you choose to, you may omit the bread & butter plate. Just be sure the entree plate is large enough to include space for a roll or bread, if that's to be included in the meal. You may omit the wine, or serve a sherry before dinner if you like, and you may omit the coffee or tea until dessert. These decisions may be due to lack of space, or simply your personal choice.

If you're serving family style, with bowls and large plates of food on the table, this offers a lot of options. For instance, you may place each person's entree plate on the table at the beginning and, if soup is the first course, a soup bowl can go on top of it. The same with the salad plate, to be removed before the main course.

✳   ✳   ✳   ✳   ✳

Going Formal

Very expensive restaurants, black tie banquets and plush cruise ships are where you might find yourself a bit challenged with formalized table settings. If you have a full range of silver and you want to plan a six or seven course dinner, you may feel the need to go full tilt. Your mother (or finishing school) may have told you the proper formalized setting pattern, which I'm sure you'll find ideal. Who am I to argue with *your* mother?

One thing though, don't do a formal setting using silver such as fish knife and fish cocktail fork, for courses that won't be offered. Obviously it doesn't make sense, and it says, "We're showing off our silver but, surprise! we don't have the food."

In the case of a cruise ship, where you have the choice of ordering anything on the menu, the waiter is suppose to remove the silver you won't be using once you've requested your menu. And, if he's alert he, or the bus boy, will remove expended silver and, if needed, add fresh ones after each course. In your home, if the affair is formalized, a good catering service ought to do the same.

While we're at it, another thing that should make the meal move smoothly, is the signal that you have finished a course. When you have definitely finished a course, place the silver you've used straight across the top of your plate. Hopefully the waiter or waitress will read your signal. However, if you wish to continue, for a pause, leave the piece of silver you are using on the right side, or at an angle at the upper right corner of the plate. By the way, a non-verbal signal used in Chinese restaurants, is that if the tea pot needs refilling, place the lid of the tea pot, on top of the pot, open or tilted.

Sometimes these things work, sometimes they don't. I find you have to *communicate* the best way applicable at the time and place…(avoiding brute force, that is). For instance, I don't care for white bread. But sometimes I find you have to "break" a waiter's or a waitress's pace in order to get their attention to your specific request. Often they may be pre-occupied, thinking of the last customer who may have given them a hard time (or they wish had given them a hard…never mind) Anyway, when ordering a sandwich or breakfast toast, to be sure the server is really paying attention, I start by asking a question: "Do you have whole wheat bread?" He or she then has to answer your question. (Hopefully you've gotten his full attention.) I then proceed to say, "Could I please have my sandwich on whole wheat toast?"

My parents were restaurateurs. Mother and father both made it clear to me early on that if you aren't given the order you requested, do not accept it. You aren't making a scene. You are probably doing the server and the restaurant a favor. If you ordered rye but got white, someone else is probably getting rye, but hates it! And, if the server hasn't figured out the mistake, he may end up having to dump the sandwich on rye to make a new one for the other guy that ordered white. In the meantime you, and possibly the other person, may have reluctantly but silently eaten the wrong sandwich and vowed never to return. But remember, be considerate and don't get mad. Getting upset only spoils it for you and for your companion. The most important thing is to enjoy your outing, the company and the ambiance.

*   *   *   *   *

Brunch

In the gay community brunch has become a social institution. I'm sure the idea must have been conceived by some maitre d' and the manager of some swank Swiss, or swish hotel. (and they were probably making out on the side…I can dream, can't I?)

Be that as it may, Gay America has adopted the art of brunch as its own. It's usually Sunday, sometimes Saturday or a holiday, not necessarily between breakfast and lunch and not necessarily a combination of the two.

It's so appealing. It can be completely informal or it can be grand…A buffet or a sit-down affair. Coming after a Saturday night out and/or a morning with a lover. Plan it for mid-morning, noon or afternoon. And, if you don't have the energy or simply can't face the kitchen, you can always take the easy way out and meet at a restaurant. It seems as though almost any eventful meal with friends, mid-day, on Saturday, Sunday or a holiday, can be called brunch. It may not be the only way to entertain gay friends, but it has certainly become one of the most popular.

*   *   *   *   *

Other Ways to Throw a Party

Planned sit-down dinners can be a big chore. But maybe you've surrounded yourself with friends who enjoy doing elaborate entertaining… hopefully not trying to out-do one another. And remember my friend, you are expected to reciprocate!

I find that to do a lot of dinners or brunches right, one has to keep the house in a fairly ready and well organized condition. But maybe you feel the need to entertain and don't want to spend a lot of time preparing. Beside, cleaning up the house may, in itself, be a major project. You might consider a reliable catering service. With a catering service you'll need to budget costs and decide whether you want to use their silver and china (extra cost) or your own. And there's the other choice: Do you want to pay to have them do the cleaning up, or are you willing to face the dirty dishes the next day?

Then there are some nice informal alternatives. There's the aforementioned brunch, or there's the out-doors approach: tossed and/or potato salad, barbecued ribs, chicken or hamburgers, buns (oh boy!) and rye bread if I'm invited, (hint, hint) wine, soft drinks and beer…very macho! Of course there's the ever-popular pot luck. The pot-luck approach is good for most gay entertaining. Why? Because with our fast pace lifestyle, many have good intentions about reciprocating hospitality, but pot-luck means reciprocity isn't required.

Of course pot-luck can take almost as much planning as doing it all yourself. It depends on the number you're inviting. My mother sent me off to the boy scouts when I was twelve. I'm not sure if she was trying to "make a man of me" or maybe, just trying to get me out of the house. Anyway, one thing that was pounded into my little head in the Boy Scouts (they didn't know I was gay) was to always "be prepared!"

So you've planned what everyone is to bring, then someone doesn't show. He, she, (or they) was to have brought an entree. With something that vital to the party a back-up entree is a must. Thank god for frozen foods and the microwave. Here, by the way, is another reason to always have some extra entrees in the freezer. At any rate, for every item (salad, vegetable, casserole, desert, etc.) have a back-up or alternative in mind. Timing is also important with pot-lucks. Have snacks and beverages available at the time your guests are to arrive. Wait about half an hour before mentally panicking because someone hasn't shown up. After a half hour if, say, the vegetables haven't arrived, pull some from the freezer and pop them in the microwave. Don't make a scene by announcing that some clod didn't show up with one of the courses.

Buffet style entertaining is nice. It's informal and it can be very color-ful. If you go that route, be sure to have large plates, or sectional paper plates, large napkins (paper's okay) and plenty of space for sitting…maybe a place for each guest at some card tables. (Memories of Mother's bridge club.)

Another style that is excellent for the buffet, pot luck or cocktail party, is the method I learned from a caterer who does both office and home parties. He called it using *vignettes*.

If you have the space and surfaces, such as side tables and, of course the dining room table, side board/buffet, etc., a dinette table (if it's actu-ally away from the kitchen preparation area)…then set up you *vignettes*. Have one for beef, chicken or turkey, and/or smoked salmon or shrimp, salads, raw vegetables and one for desserts. At these *vignettes* you might also have an appropriate wine, beer, coffee, tea, etc. It's especially nice to have a flower arrangement or flowering plant as a back drop at a few of these little centers.

This plan makes it easy for guests to move about and to mingle rather than having them all assembling in one place (the horrible chow line-up) for the food orgy. By the way, if furniture and space requires that you place all the food on one table, arrange that guests are able to serve themselves from both sides of the table, if at all possible.

Here are some other ideas for throwing parties that suggest interest-ing atmosphere and food possibilities:

Christmas Tree Trimming Party. And guests are asked to bring one useless "white elephant" gift, wrapped. To be exchanged, or possibly use them as gifts for charity.

Video Party. (Announce the film to be shown.)

Chinese New Year Party.

Fourth of July Party.

Mardi Gras or Halloween Party. (Because of the need for costumes you should invite guests at least a month in advance.)

It's Spring Party.

Birthday Party.

Anniversary Party. (You've been a couple for 5, 10 or 20+ years.) If you don't wish to have gifts, say: "no gifts please." But if anyone brings one, receive it graciously at the door, but quietly put it to one side so as not to embarrass the others. And, if you *haven't* stipulated "no gifts," then it's nice to have small token gifts available to hand out as they are leaving…Again, without fanfare.

Another note about parties: Sometimes they can get loud and late. Naturally, you don't want to alienate your neighbors, or worse, get raided. So, if you think this just might be a noisy group, let your closest neighbors (especially in condos or apartments) know that you plan to have a party, and "please let us know if we're getting too loud." This way they probably won't complain. But if they do, hopefully they'll call you before calling the police.

*　　　*　　　*　　　*　　　*

Give and Take

About "thank you's" and reciprocating: Don't accept invitations, enjoy your friend's hospitality (parties take some work—they don't just happen) then forget it…Even if it's a "pot-luck," call the next day to express your appreciation. I was pleased to read in the terribly hip GQ *Magazine*, that they suggested you send a handwritten thank you note when you accept the hospitality of someone like, say, your boss. So it's your close friends or family…a note of thanks is always appropriate. Good manners and good sense tell us we owe it to anyone who extends their hospitality, to return the favor, or to extend our appreciation in some way. Look at it this way: Would you accept service in a restaurant without leaving a tip? Like tipping, reciprocation and extending thanks to the host, is an unwritten courtesy.

So maybe you have a small bachelor apartment and it's impossible to throw parties (for more than the two of you). Then, whenever you accept an invitation, ask what you can contribute to the festivities or bring a simple house gift or bottle of good wine. And afterwards, don't forget to call or send a card or note of thanks.

If "the shoe is on the other foot" and you have a close friend who tends to forget, or seems unaware, I feel you owe it to him or her, to start the ball rolling. You know the size of his apartment or house, so if you know he is gregarious, but doesn't seem to know how to entertain, suggest, "How about inviting Bill and Joe over to your place next Sunday? I'll bring the entree if you'll provide the place and the salad." (Some people need a nudge.)

Then, of course, there is always the exception to all of this. I believe that once you've gotten to know someone fairly well, but you find you have nothing in common except your mutual interest in same-sex relationships, it might be time to bring the relationship to a comfortable (or screeching) halt. Unless you both enjoy debating when you find you simply don't agree on most topics, don't try to make something out of a relationship that has no friendship qualities. Life's too short to waste with people you're uncomfortable being around. And remember, that goes for both of you.

*   *   *   *   *

More on Party Planning

As usual, the gay community is way ahead of all the others in party trends. (Aren't I ethnocentric?....or is that *homocentric*?) Anyway...

Because of our fast pace of life, it is becoming more acceptable to be spontaneous about throwing a bash. And, gays have been entertaining spontaneously for ages. There's nothing unusual about getting a call from Mike and Jim saying, "That hunk we met in New

Zealand is visiting this weekend and we'd love to have you drop in for drinks and a light buffet." Then of course there is that wild single friend who wants you to meet (show off) his latest trick…"Come on over for an informal brunch on Sunday so you can meet David." (*Another* one !?)

But some things, like the special theme parties, are a bigger hit if you give advance notice and do some basic planning.

*   *   *   *   *

A Party Check-list

1. Plan the guest list and send invitations at least two weeks in advance. Give more notice if it's holiday season, Halloween or some other extra-special event. If you plan to mix the group, with lesbians and gays or homosocial straights mixed in, have some ice-breaker things to do, especially mixer or get-acquainted type games. But do consider the sensitivities of a mixed group, and make sure the entertainment doesn't embarrass anyone or make them feel out of place.

2. If you're asking ten or so, avoid asking just singles. Sprinkle the group with some couples. It'll do the couples good to get out among the boys, and hopefully they are good role models.

3. If you know someone who enjoys playing the guitar, or such, ask ahead of time if he or she would mind playing a few pieces. But remember, if he or she is a professional entertainer you really must offer to pay the fee. If paid entertainment seems a little too pricey for your budget, don't hesitate to set up some nice background music on the CD player. At any rate, don't allow the music to be so loud it dominates the party…they didn't come for a concert.

4. A week in advance write out your shopping list. Cross the items off as you get them (or already have them).

5. Don't forget the flowers and your outfit. Good color is a nice factor. Fresh flowers especially add to the festivities and decor. But don't have centerpieces at a sit-down affair that people can't see over. You and the colors in your home combine to create your own special ambiance.

6. Buy some fresh paper hand towels for the bathroom (or be sure to have enough fresh hand towels available). If you're having a buffet, be sure to get large colorful (or color coordinated) napkins. Naturally for the sit-down meal you'll want to be sure to have enough linen, or fancy paper napkins.

7. Don't forget to warn close (or invite homosocial) neighbors so they won't be unduly alarmed if the group gets loud.

8. Depending on the size of your abode, it's nice to have a separate table (or bar) for drinks and another for dessert. Some like the dessert at the table for a sit-down affair. But I like to make a break so that people can move after dinner, then enjoy dessert in the living room or, on a warm day, on the patio.

9. A day in advance prepare some hors d'oeuvre, and anything that can be frozen, and properly refrigerated for freshness.

10. When buying wine, with a large group you don't need to get expensive types. Your favorite house wines, by the jug, are fine, using glass or crystal decanters. But, of course, if you are a wine connoisseur it's nice to show off appropriate vintages. For mixed drinks you can usually plan a bourbon, scotch, gin and vermouth and, of course, your soda waters. Generally at cocktail type parties, on the average, people will consume 2 to 3 mixed drinks or glasses of wine per person. You can get about 16-17 shots per fifth. Don't forget, most states now say that you are partly responsible if

someone has an auto accident because you've been generous with your liquor. Plan food after drinks or well interspersed.

11. Be sure there are enough seats for everyone. If all else fails, some huge pillows on the floor may be required. And, of course, if you're running out of seating surfaces, *you* will volunteer to use a large pillow or simply stay in motion.

12. Plan to have everything "at the ready" at least an hour before guests are expected. Have drinks, mixes, wine, etc., plus things to nibble, ready for those who are prompt. Get everything picked up.

13. At least an hour in advance, plan to cater to yourself. Lay out your clothes, shave, shower (or better yet, take a relaxing bath) splash on your favorite after-shave, dress, and...*voila*...the elegant host (hostess?)!

Then, as Mother would say: "Now it's time to make yourself useful as well as ornamental."

When the guests arrive, try to have things at a point where you don't have to spend time in the kitchen. Be sure you or your partner greet the guests at the door with a warm welcome. A hug is in order (unless it's your boss who's straight, or an employee, and his wife). After you've greeted them and taken any wraps (or whatever they're willing to remove) if they're not familiar with the group, be sure each guest meets one or two other people. If there's time, try to remember something special about each guest which can enhance personal introductions, like, "Jerry, I'd like you to meet Bill. Bill's the fabulous tennis player John and I met at the club." Or, "Jerry and Mike, I'd like you to meet Bob. Bob is the great travel agent that planned our cruise last year."

By the way, while we're on introductions, if for some reason Jerry and Mike aren't into cruising (on ships), think of something else like: "Bob is a computer whiz." It's just something to get the conversation started...the icebreaker idea.

Basically you're giving your guests an opportunity to pick up on items. When there's a break in the conversation, or if none has started, offer the newcomer a drink or show him to the fixings. It's always nice for a guest to have something in his hand if he's feeling self-conscious.

As the host I find it's a good rule to have one mild drink, if you like, then stick to the mixes only. See that everyone is well cared for, but *you* mustn't get bombed!

For couples I strongly recommend cooperative advance planning. Who's going to vacuum, dust, buy the groceries and all, and who's going to cook, tend bar, greet at the door, mix and converse, while the other one does the last minute kitchen-to-table duties?

Don't leave things to the last, hectic, minute. And *do not*, due to the inevitable strain, get upset with each other in front of guests, making them wish they hadn't accepted your invitation. We all have our little domestic spats; but no one enjoys witnessing someone else's!

Your guests are there because they want to enjoy your company and the pleasant memories of your hospitality. Good luck. And, have a ball!

9

Party Time Post-script

After reading Dr. Wayne Dyer's book, *Erroneous Zones*, I find that I need a little self-correction. I'm making the assumption here that it's okay to pick a paragraph from his book to illustrate a few points. This is from the chapter "Breaking the Barrier of Convention," which also adds his note: "There are no rules, laws or traditions that apply universally…including this one."

Under the title "Etiquette as a Should," Dr. Dyer states: "Etiquette is a beautiful example of useless and unhealthy enculturation. Think of all the little meaningless rules you've been encouraged to adopt simply because Emily Post, Amy Vanderbilt, or Abigail van Buren has so written. Eat your corn on the cob this way, always wait for the hostess to start before eating, introduce the man to the woman, sit on that side of the Church at a wedding, tip this, wear that, use these words. Don't consult yourself; look it up in the book. While good manners are certainly appropriate—they simply entail consideration for other people—about ninety percent of all the etiquette guidelines are meaningless rules that were composed arbitrarily at one time. There is no proper way for you; there is only what you decide is right for you—as long as you don't make it hard for others to get along. You can choose how you'll introduce people, what you'll tip, what you'll wear, how you'll speak, where you'll sit, how you'll eat, and so on, strictly on the basis of what you want. Anytime you fall into the trap of 'what should I wear,' or 'how should I do it,' you've given up a chunk of yourself. I'm not making a case here for being a social rebel since that would be a form of approval seeking through nonconformity, but rather this is a plea for being self-rather than other-directed in the everyday running of your life. Being true to yourself means being devoid of the need for an external support system."

In many ways I agree with Dr. Dyer and, as we all know, in our gay lifestyle, we *have* established many of our own "rights" and "wrongs." If we are finally comfortable with ourselves then, hopefully, we have learned how to get along within the gay community. Certainly "The Book of Etiquette," is not our Bible, no matter who the editor might be.

However, I believe that most adults have learned to get along with others simply because they have had parents or role-models who have given them some direction....To feel that what they are doing is not totally weird. In other words, in agreeing with Dr. Dyer (and I thoroughly enjoy his writings and his philosophy) I take exception by saying that it is helpful to have some guidelines on how to "get along" in society as a whole. So whether you're a "social rebel" or not, I hope that my suggestions on etiquette will help to make you feel comfortable both in or out of the gay community, and especially that you'll feel comfortable with your Mr. Right.

10

Caring for the Body

Mother always said, "Good health is not a God-given right; you have to work at it." Okay, lets admit it. Very few of us are "Mr. Gorgeous Body." And most of us have our little quirks. Are you skinny or overweight? Do you smoke or do you drink a little too much?

Well, let's set some goals for ourselves. Make three lists.

The first is that of your goals in the direction of an attractive body: *Achievements for the next twelve months.* Or, maybe you can push yourself and make it six months. In any case, when trying to reach these goals, avoid any negatives and continually reassure yourself that you are on your way in reaching these goals. Remember, this list is for *your body.* Don't over do it. Be realistic. For instance, if you are 100 pounds over weight, you may not accomplish the dreamed of body-perfect in six months without adversely effecting your health. It may be a cop-out, but if you are considerably over weight, *see a doctor for guidelines.*

Far better than quick weight-loss programs is a sensible properly balanced diet on a continuing habit forming basis and a consistent exercise program.

The second list is "How To." Here you should go hog-wild. Don't hold back. List all the services and special assistance available from various health clubs. Shop around. There are many well supervised programs just for this purpose. Also list other programs that may help you control your smoking and/or drinking. Then start a process of elimination, to use the best program(s) you have found.

The third list is a very critical self-analysis. List all problems, even if you feel they are almost impossible to correct.

But if they're practically, or totally, impossible to correct, like baldness, impaired hearing, excess tallness, shortness or unique physical defect, save these items for the section on mental health, (Healthy or Worried Sick).

Now that you've listed all the problems, go back and be sure you are pulling each of these up for the challenge with your goal settings. Or, if they are in the practically impossible area, you may want to attack them first, before you've tackled your physical goals. This is up to you. Into procrastination? You have a strong will…conquer those buggers!

Get involved in a regular health program now, whether you pay for it or simply do it on your own schedule. Personally I find that if I pay for it and put it on my regular schedule, like going to the health spa every Monday, Wednesday and a weekend day, I'll do it. But if I leave it on "when I get around to it on my own time," I get lazy and put it off forever. No matter what the plan, do no less than a half hour work out at least three times each week.

Most people should have a physical exam no less than once a year. If you can't afford it, you may be able to get at least a blood test at a county health facility without charge. Also, if you're sexually active, even if you practice safe sex, go to an HIV/AIDs center and get tested!

I recommend that you find a doctor who is gay, or has a thorough understanding, and is accepting of our life-style. If you don't know of one, get a referral from a friend, or you can usually find one through the Doctors for Human Rights organization. If you can't locate one of those dedicated people, call your nearest Gay and Lesbian Community Center, usually in the major metro areas, and ask if they can suggest such a doctor in your community. If it's more convenient to write to a gay center, be sure to enclose a postage paid return envelope. I'm suggesting a doctor because you really need more than just a blood test to be sure your body is functioning at its best.

Take your problems and health goals list to your doctor. Let him or her know you are serious about getting in the pink. Most doctors are delighted to assist and make suggestions to those who have gone to the trouble of a serious self analysis.

One note of caution: If the doctor is quick to write out a prescription for pills as the end-all answer, without any consideration to diet or exercise and/or reduction of smoking or drinking, then I would get the name of another doctor from one of the sources I've suggested.

Remember, there is no law that says you must stay with one doctor from here to eternity. Your good health is far more important than the ego of a doctor who practices questionable medicine, such as, take pills and have an operation at the drop of a hat.

While we're on the subject of good health…

Eat natural, unprocessed foods, as regularly as possible. When you want something to munch on between meals, make it fruit or vegetables. Avoid fried foods and foods with excessive sugar…in general, junk food. Red meats should be kept to a minimum (if at all) and fatty foods should be avoided. Don't eat a heavy meal late in the evening, unless you plan to burn it off by dancing most of the night away. And, as my father used to say: "remember your *after breakfast*." In other words, make a habit of going to the toilet every morning. If I find myself missing this regularity, I take a prune after dinner. It works for me. Hope it does for you, as well.

If you don't have a regular physical fitness program, do at least ten minutes of exercise daily to work up a sweat and get your heart muscle pumping. If you aren't into bulging muscles, establish a program of push-ups, set-ups, long walks and light jogging in the fresh air. Don't lay flat when doing sit-ups...bend your knees. If you have back problems, and a very large percentage of adults do, consult a chiropractor or doctor before putting any strain on your back. By the way, if you go to a chiropractor, don't let him or her hook you on a long time continuous treatment, unless you really want and need that. Just be sure you continue the exercises recommended by your chiropractor or your physician.

If you jog, here are a few pointers. Do wear well fitted, cushioned running shoes. Otherwise you could be doing your body more harm than good. If you run on a street, run on the side facing traffic. It's sad to note that many joggers and runners have been hit by cars because they didn't see them coming, and/or the driver didn't see the runner until it was too late. Don't run in areas where the air is poor and/or there is car exhaust. Deep breathing of smoke and carbon monoxide is harmful to your lungs.

Mother always said, "shower or bathe every day, whether you need it or not." I don't know why that's so important, but it is a pleasant habit. Of course there are those who get turned on by the "he-man" sweaty smell. If your lover is one of those, at least take a shower each morning before facing the outside world..."whether you need it or not."

Don't forget to use a mildly scented (or no-scent) under-arm deodorant. While we're on the subject of odors, here are some tips on choosing a fragrance and after shave.

Those who push the sale of perfumes (much like those who sell high fashion clothes) will tell you it isn't "in" to stick with one scent. They suggest you vary your fragrances, depending on what you wear and where you're going, such as plush dinner and the opera versus an outing with the Great Outdoors. Maybe so, it's up to your interests and tastes. Personally, I like keeping life as simple as possible, which is probably a reflection on the state of my mind. Anyway, if you're anything like me, and you'd prefer easy decisions (especially in those blurry eyed early morning hours) you'll find a faithful fragrance and stick with it until something more to your liking comes along.

So how do we choose? Of course there are a thousand different elegant brands (along with elegant prices) and fancy names. Let's see what scent category you're looking for.

Three of the most popular he-man scents are: 1. Green and woodsy (natural outdoors), 2. Spicy, such as clove, ginger or cinnamon, and 3. Fruity (no remarks please) such as lemon, lime or orange. A little more distinctive and exotic are the blends such as: 1. Oriental or smoky musk-ambergris, opium, the leathers, and sandalwood; 2. Modern blends (or aldehydes) such as Chanel, Rochas, Arpage or Aviance (there are probably hundreds more being produced right now, but you've got the picture); and 3. Florals and floral bouquets, taken from specific flowers or blends of buds. Take your pick. Hopefully this gives you an idea of the scent you might like people to remember you by.

As for choosing your preference at the store; decide on one or two. Ask the sales person (where are they when you need them?) or check for yourself from the selection at a well stocked department store. You don't have to buy right away. Take your time and enjoy making a choice of which one you'd like to live with…(not the salesman, the cologne.)

The best way to try them is to settle on no more than three…two if possible. Dab or spray a little on different parts of your arms. Wait at least ten minutes while you're shopping or browsing. Then check the scents on your arm and you'll get a better idea of what "grows" on you. Have a good time.

Here are a few other personal care hints for your consideration. If your skin seems sensitive to alcohol and/or tends to be very dry, then try an emulsion after shave or balm, as some call it. Want your after shave to be extra refreshing? Try storing it in the refrigerator. But be careful. It doesn't go well on salads.

Periodically try a facial scrub to remove dry cells. This uncovers fresh healthy skin just under the surface. And, from time to time, you might rejuvenate your face with a skin conditioner after washing up before bed…that is if you have nothing special planned in the bed .

Of course, brush your teeth after breakfast, and before bedtime brush and floss. Ask a good friend or relative if you are inclined to have bad breath. Don't be offended by an honest reply. Some people have halitosis without realizing it. If you have such a problem, brush after each meal and brush off your tongue as well. Also, use a mouth wash regularly…especially before going out for the evening or every few hours if you work close to the public or fellow employees.

The *Unofficial Gay Manual*, by Kevin Dilallo and Jack Krumholtz, has some especially good pointers in the chapter, "Someday My Prince Will Come." They did some research and found certain things that are turnoffs to most (not all) gay men: Femmes—"If I wanted a woman, I'd be straight." Attitude—"Seems most men prefer guys with their feet on the ground to those with their noses in the air." Self-absorption—"…try to show some, if only a passing interest in others." Bad Bodies—"A gym membership really could pay off, but only if you spend at least as much time on the weights as you do in the showers. "Unsightly Body Hair—"…back, ear and nose hair seem to be the most problematic." Smoking—"Kissing an ash tray is not something most gay men find stimulating." Cologne—"Apparently the excessive use of cologne is more widespread than originally thought." No Sense of Humor—"A cardinal sin in the gay world." Poor Taste in Clothes—"Who said gay men are superficial?"

Speaking of smoking, if you smoke you will probably continue to have a breath problem. Inhaled cigarette smoke can't be corrected by simply brushing your teeth. If you're concerned because you continue to have bad breath, you'd better see your doctor. This could indicate a health problem.

As they say, "see your dentist twice a year." This means in *his office, about your teeth*! I think you'll find that it's cheaper than dental insurance to have your teeth cleaned at the dentist's every six months.

Also, brushing with baking soda once a week helps keep your smile squeaky clean.

How about hair (not in the teeth) on your head and body? Starting at the top, if you aren't satisfied with your current shampoo, ask your barber if your hair is oily or too dry. Then find a shampoo that will help balance the hair and scalp condition. Whether you shampoo daily or a couple of times a week is up to you. But if you smoke, I'd suggest you wash your hair with every shower. Hair picks up the smoke smell which is a turn-off to many.

Bald or balding? Stop worrying about it! This is the sign of a father image to many. Anyway, if someone judges you by the quantity of hair on your head, your wealth or lack of it, or the shade of your skin…need I say more?

Moving right along,…downward that is. If you have considerable body hair it's a good idea to keep your neck, shaved. However, when you wear sport shirts it could be appealing to let a little of the "rug" show on your chest. It gives those who might be interested, a preview of coming attractions.

Back to your list of healthy goals for the next six to twelve months. Zero-in on a specific goal you want to accomplish, such as loosing twenty pounds and/or developing the abs and biceps. Get into your health plan in any way you wish…a healthy diet plus that regular health spa schedule, regular jogging and/or long energetic walks.

Each morning take an extra ten minutes or so, where you won't be disturbed, say in the bedroom or in the bathroom (with the seat lid down). Sit up straight. Lay your hands (open, not closed fists) on your knees. Close your eyes and make a personal statement of affirmation, such as, "I am slim and I have handsome biceps." Or any other short positive statement about what you have as a healthy goal, like: "I work relaxed and I get along with my co-workers." Now, *very slowly* count to twenty. Don't allow anything to distract you. Sitting up straight, completely relaxed, when you get to twenty (or if you wish—up to forty) think about your positive statement and repeat it. Good. Now *slowly* count backward. At number eleven repeat your statement. Continue counting back to one. Stand up, take several slow deep breaths and, if possible wash your face with cold water. This exercise is called *depth conditioning* which is a type of self hypnosis. The affirmation is placed in your subconscious. You've given yourself a strong personal statement that will be with you all day to help you with your positive plan for progress.

I doubt that you can lie to yourself. Look into the mirror. Smile. You have many fantastic qualities and attributes! Maybe you haven't yet reduced to the perfect slim body or added to the biceps all you'd like. But you are certainly working on your program daily. And, before you know it, those statements are coming true!

Now, while we're in the area of *depth conditioning*, you may already be familiar with other disciplines in the unity of mind and body self control. Whether or not you have studied into these subjects, you might consider any one of several books and/or classes that I'm sure you would enjoy, depending on your personal interests and inclinations. Should you prefer a scientific approach, check into *biofeedback*, or a Christian based philosophy such as *Science of Mind*; then there are the eastern based philosophies such as *Zen Buddhism* (in particular, its practice of *meditation*) as well as the physical/mental exercises like *yoga, tai chi* and *judo*.

Whatever plan you might select, remember to walk straight (better yet, proud!) hold your head erect and your chest forward.... .You're terrific! Keep up the good work. And when that affirmative statement is accomplished to your high standards, go on to other goals. Man, there's no stopping you now!

11

Dressed and Undressed

Mother use to say: "How you dress shows how you feel about yourself."

Consider your reasons for dressing the way that you do. That is aside from taking pride in being a part of the community or, maybe, a "Castro Clone."

I delight in visiting the San Francisco Castro. And after all, a lot of fashion began in the city by the Golden Gate. Look at the huge international trade in Levis.

Why do you dress the part, or in some particular style? Consider:

1. Your need to impress others

2. Showing your financial ability or position

3. Dressing in keeping with your age group

4. Showing off your physique

5. Clothes that compliment your coloring

6. Response to weather conditions

7. Dressing for activities, i.e.: school, sports, social functions.

Doesn't your wardrobe change with the season? Maybe there's a need to impress people, for the sake of maintaining or improving your career.

So forget the hang-up about feeling guilty because you spent a small fortune on that leather jacket and those chaps. There's nothing wrong with feeling the part when you're trying to impress that special someone with what a hunk you are!

By the way, let's not forget where the money is made…No, not cruising Santa Monica Blvd. What to wear at business and semi-business events is very important. Now this may sound a bit old-fashioned, but I encourage men to wear ties at work if any of your peers do the same. In addition to that, you might do one better and help set the fashion standard. If you consider yourself any kind of a professional in your field, remember, people notice what you're wearing.

Then there's the trendy "corporate casual." It's more than merely a sport coat and slacks. As we speak I'm seeing men with turtle neck or heavy T-shirts under a stylish sport shirt, plus slacks, loafers and of course, a jacket or sports coat. Naturally color coordination is important; I especially like shades of tone-on-tone.

When it comes to really looking the part…call it "business-drag" if you want, don't you get a charge out of knowing you look just right for the occasion? Okay, so I'm not the most virile looking stud at the dinner party or the bar, but by God, I feel great and therefore I have more self confidence.

Like wearing an after-shave that compliments your personality, when choosing colors to wear, consider how those colors compliment or accentuate your hair, eyes and skin color. I know a PR man who has blue eyes and black hair, graying at the sideburns. He invariably wears a blue tie, or a tie with blue in it. He'll be wearing a blue, black or gray suite. He is a knock out! He may not be the brightest of businessmen. But the ladies give him just about all the time he wants and the men …ah hum, well they certainly respect him. In fact I think some of the straight ones are a little jealous.

Whether you buy there or not, go to a well established expensive department store and/or men's store. You'll get some ideas of what is really sound and smart fashion. Then, if you have the time and inclination, go to a less expensive store or an outlet and find comparable clothes at better prices. But do be careful of "trendy" clothes. Unless you have buckets of money to spend on such things, you can be buying clothes that will be "out" in a few months.

Avoid over-dressing....Don't try to outdo others with "flashy" attire. By the way, be careful about showing off expensive looking clothes when you travel. Expensive clothes and jewelry make you a target for pick-pockets and other thieves in airports and large cities. This is the reason you'll see wealthy and prominent people often wearing jeans and very casual sport clothes as they take their seats in first class. They enjoy dressing well, but they know that airports and walking in even expensive parts of the city are not the places to impress the public.

Talking about impressing people, I'm so cheap that when a good pair of Speedo swim trunks I really liked, became a sickly bleached green, instead of buying a new pair, I decided to dye them black. Before taking a trip to my friend's place on Maui, I went to the store and bought a bottle of black fabric dye.

At home I dyed the swim trunks, dried them out, and put them in my bag. At Maui, my friend lived a couple of blocks from the beach. One afternoon he told me he wanted me to meet a local friend, so he was having him over for drinks, then we'd go out to dinner. I asked Don if I'd have time to run down to the beach for a short swim? "Sure," he said, "Jack will be here in about two hours, so take your time." Off I went to the beach in those hot looking black Speedos. After a dip in the ocean, some cruising and a little sunning, I started back to Don's. I was thinking how great I must look here on a beach in Hawaii, wearing those sexy black swim trunks. Very slowly, I noticed a pickup truck coming along. The driver pulled over and asked if I was Don's friend and would I like a lift. Well! Mother told me about strangers offering lifts, so I automatically said "it's only a couple of blocks, I'll walk, thank you." (Besides, he wasn't really my type, and who knows what else might come along?) When I got back to Don's, sure enough there was his friend's truck. I went in to shower and change into some fresh clothes. Taking off my *hot* black swim trunks, I looked down and, oh my God....My legs were streaked with black dye! What a terrible impression that must have made. I guess this goes to show that I shouldn't be so cheap. Yes Mother, I hear you: "When all else fails dear, read the directions!" If I had read the directions completely, I would have seen that I was suppose to have rinsed the trunks in cold water to let the dye set. Certainly I wouldn't have had the dye setting, like black varicose veins, streaked down my legs.

*   *   *   *   *

When speaking of buying clothes and taking trips, I'd be negligent if I didn't point out a certain matter of economics. As soon as you have a regular income and a permanent address, you'll be "flattered" with invitations to accept offers of various credit cards. They'll be so impressive in their gold and platinum shades. They'll make you feel like "a million" as you flash them to the reservationist, the cashier or the waiter. And guess what? As long as the charge is approved, these people could care less what your card says or looks like. As you know, financial institutions are making these offers for one reason, and one reason alone...to make a profit every time you use their card. Go ahead and have a credit card. But don't let those already rich financial institutions get even richer off of you. If you don't budget yourself and pay off your card charges *each month*, you are paying the highest possible interest rate on your balance. What ever you do, find a way to pay off your charges each month, but don't let a balance due carry forward...it's like throwing your hard earned money down the drain!

12

Healthy or Worried Sick

I'll never forget Mother's cryptic remark: "If you live a fast life and die young, you will have a handsome corpse." Some still seem to be striving to be young and beautiful all of their *short* lives, while living on the wild side, but soon they'll be dead! No thanks; I love life! In addition to the vital rule of safe-sex, here are a few items to consider.

Don't overlook water. No, not water sports, sweety! Out of the tap or bottled, water is probably our body's greatest ally. It helps fight disease and preserves that fresh balance for a longer life. Believe it or not, it even helps burn off fat. At least we can do one thing to the extreme and it's healthy…Drink lots of water!

I have a home-made remedy to shorten colds. When you get the feeling that you might have a cold coming on, head for the water fountain and prepare to flush out the body with that good old H_2O. Start by taking several glasses of water…say 3 or 4. Naturally you'll have to go urinate before long. Hold it! Before going to the john take another glass of water. The next time you get the urge, do the same. Keep this up for as long as the ache or cold persists. For one thing, you'll be so tired of this you'll probably psyche yourself out of whatever you're trying to get. Like the doctor said, "drink lots of liquids, take an aspirin (or non-aspirin pain reliever) and get plenty of rest."

We've all been heavily exposed to the news and information on HIV and AIDs. The epidemic has taken so many of the lives of those who we love and those who have contributed so much to modern civilization. It was once *our problem*. But finally even heterosexuals are getting the message. It is urgent that we all practice safe sex!

Of course each one of us feels that we understand the workings and idiosyncrasies of our own body. No? As they say, "join the club." Have you considered what is and what isn't safe when it comes to homosexual intercourse? Can I use Viagra? Sex toys? Can I be promiscuous and still be "clean" when I find the perfect mate? Will a condom or oral sex protect me against AIDs?

I'm very pleased to report that an excellent book has recently been published that is perfectly blunt about all the questions you've wanted to ask. It's an in-depth dissertation that helps us understand our body, and it makes for better communication with our doctor: *The Ins and Outs of Gay Sex*, written by Stephen E. Goldstone, M.D. (published by Dell Publishing, 1999). Get it! It's an investment in good health.

Looking into the whys and wherefores of health problems, we might ask ourselves, "which came first, the chicken or the egg?" By the way, that egg was caused by the brain. The brain stimulated the body and the body produced the egg....Okay, I admit it, I'm *not* a brilliant biochemist!

The point is that if you want to get to the root of a physical problem, your best bet is to go back to the brain.

Homosexuals are afflicted with physical problems that have been caused by anxiety more often than by heredity. Say you find yourself over-eating, over-drinking, chain smoking, having frequent headaches, unaccountable muscular problems, frequent outbreaks of herpes, or other skin irritations, etc.….Your doctor may help with one of the "miracle drugs," or he may refer you to a psychologist or psychiatrist.

However, if you feel your problem is based on a psychosis and you want to go direct, mental health counselors with knowledge of gay problems, can be found advertising in many gay publications. Of course, advertising in those publications does not guarantee that they have the expertise you may need. You may want to check at a gay community center or be referred by other professionals.

Alcohol and drug abuse are often brought on as a response to other emotional problems. The aggravation is often caused by the anxiety from the necessity to maintain a two-faced existence in order to survive.

If you have any of these emotional disorders, it has been proven that psychological counseling can greatly reduce or eliminate other medical and hospital costs. If your're fortunate enough not to be carrying any of this emotional luggage…that's great!

But we are, after all, in a gay minority community where we may not feel comfortable as a part of the straight society. And some may even feel disassociated from both groups.

Perhaps you are a gay male who is less than 5 feet 5 inches tall. Maybe you are black, brown, or have impaired hearing or sight. In other words you do not fit the image of the advertised so-called "all-American" WASP. Excuse me, but that WASP image exclusivity is bullshit!

Listen, my friend—Be aware that you are a part of a special 10+ percent of humanity that is helping (without wars and famine) to control a rapidly increasing human population. You have a rare ability to empathize with the less fortunate, yet you enjoy a capability to create great art and to enhance the environment in which we all live. Yes, I'd say that you even have a *responsibility* to live up to the high standards of those gays and lesbians who came before you.

Homophobes, and others who do not understand this, should be pitied…though it may be difficult to muster that much compassion!

Due to a serious illness in my early twenties, I became bald. And I learned to live with it. I believe that, to allow such characteristics to further bring us down is to give up without a fight!

Just as I ask you to see the special qualities and intrinsic beauty in others, I implore you now to acknowledge the unique and wonderful values you hold within yourself. As human beings we all have extraordinary qualities. Those who lose their sight, their hearing or their limbs; learn, in order to survive, how to strengthen and enhance their remaining capabilities.

Personally I have found many, in both gay and straight society, who have a fascination and even a desire for bald men. Among my friends I know of many who pay absolutely no attention to a person's height. Many have an attraction to the very tall, or those who are shorter, and those with very hairy or have mostly hairless bodies. Fortunately, independent thinking and the desire for the unusual has become not only acceptable, but even admirable in recent years. I say, thank heavens, it's about time!

Enjoy being the person *you* are! Accept others, and especially yourself, for the unique qualities that are there, not for what you wish were there.

13

Considerations on Coupling

I was in the Army. I was not there voluntarily. Maybe that's why, basically, I have a disdain for those who make rules for the sake of conformity. Especially those who get their ego kicks by enforcing *their* rules upon others.

But the society's accepted rules of etiquette are a two way street...they can be very helpful when it comes to our human relationships. You may know of people who are simply a "turn-off" because, to put it mildly, they act like idiots when it comes to getting along with others! If they want to be accepted by a group or, for that matter, by individuals, they should become acquainted with the group's social behavior, to follow their leads and thus, fit in.

It is these unspoken rules that help us find the way through the otherwise complicated pattern of social behavior in any given community or country.

Couple relationships are simply made up of two people, right? And a couple relationship should be made up of individuals who both, *both*, have a feeling of self worth. Each must have a feeling of being not only worthwhile, but lovable. First off you, number one, must be yourself!

Otherwise number two won't know if, or who, he is really loving. Hopefully you know your own strong points. You know why someone else should like or, hopefully, love you. Now, to yourself, you need to recognize *your own* goals, wants, qualities and feelings.

I am sure that one of your most important needs is to be loved, and to love in return. You can be sure that this is his first priority as well.

When you do find the right partner, you'll want to inspire these feelings in him, if they aren't already apparent. You will find your communication and your relationship will be a delight as you become more aware of each other. These feelings will be good for both of you, as you will both be receiving the most vital emotion of your life: mutual love.

Relating to each other, with openness and honesty, you will learn more about him and about yourself. Then too, allow your partner, and yourself, opportunities for privacy. This has nothing to do with ones desire, or lack of desire, for mutual love. This is a very natural way for an individual to react, on his own time, to his highs and his lows. It is wonderful to be together; but each of us came into this world alone, and ultimately each must face the reality that we leave the same way…alone.

If that certain sex appeal seems to leave each of you now and then, don't panic. Allow a little time to pass, then get to know each other again. It is said that, in a period of eight years, each of us completely changes, both emotionally and physically. It doesn't happen overnight. But gradually it does happen. So, if things seem a bit dull, just remember that you'll both be different people within eight years.

Don't be afraid to gently verbalize your feelings, your understandings as well as your misunderstandings. Those feelings may be hard to express, for fear of hurting the other person, or for fear of rejection. But far worse than a negative reaction is the dangerous inner pain of not allowing your partner to know your true feelings, or bearing a grudge and allowing small misunderstandings to develop out of proportion.

Say that your mate makes a statement out of anger or out of emotional hurt. Your first reaction might be to put him down or to react with an abrupt opinion. Stop! Think a minute and restate the problem in a way that says: "I understand and I appreciate your feelings. I'm willing to listen and to empathize with you." Don't blast back an answer you may later regret. And don't silently avoid the problem. Make it clear that you want to understand and you want to help solve the problem. Sometimes when we hear our problem re-stated by another person, we can come to a clearer understanding on how to cope with it on our own terms...that's the best person-to-person therapy.

If there is a conflict, after you've had a chance to give it some thought, (giving full consideration to the other person's point of view) verbalize the problem as you see it without being judgmental. Make it clear that you have considered it from his point of view. Such as "I realize that you hate cooking; but I find I'm spending more time in the kitchen than I really care to. Could we discuss a plan for alternate cooking days, or possibly a trade-off for other chores?"

If your partner doesn't seem in a very good mood at the time, then ask for a later time when it can be discussed. Reassure him that you know how he feels about cooking (or what ever the problem might be) and that you'd just like to discuss alternatives.

Then, when you do have a chance to discuss the problem, remember to try and put yourself in his place during the conversation. When you've both explored the options, try arriving at an agreeable conclusion. Briefly verbalize your mutual agreement and, hopefully, you will have solved the problem.

I know it is not all that simple. But give the plan a try. It's far better than letting a minor disagreement grow and eat away at your insides. You may feel like you're giving up your own ego for his sake. But if you practice this method a few times, let me assure you that he will catch on. Love is the world's most powerful positive force. Let it work for you!

In addition to the mental and emotional aspects of your love relationship, your verbal encounters will help bind another aspect of your relationship which cements you as a team...it's called *trust*. As you establish this trust in your love relationship, you'll find a wonderful security in being yourself, and in being yourselves together.

You'll have trust in your partner, and you'll know that each of you is going to change with age—that you will both seek out and enjoy how the other person changes and matures from day to day.

This may all sound a bit overwhelming. Don't worry, you'll get use to it...you'll love it! There is one basic rule that makes any relationship (gay or straight) run smoothly. That rule is honesty. First, be honest with yourself. Then work to be confident in knowing that you can be fully honest with your partner. If you aren't use to this type of openness, this may take time to get use to. Keep trying, and try to make honesty a habit. Love comes naturally, and it grows when honesty is at its foundation.

We all know that life, and love, is not filled with watching beautiful sunsets and smelling nature's exquisite flowers. Love in this life is accepting the world and the universe as they are. That is truly being one with what the infinite has created. Love allows you to truly enjoy life...especially when someone enjoys it with you.

That world with which we are one, includes volcanoes, storms, and earthquakes. They may seem insurmountable at the time. But when those storms in this world have passed, as in our relationships, there will always be flowers that bloom, colorful sunsets and spectacular sunrises! The beautiful islands of the Pacific did not appear without volcanic eruptions and rainstorms. With human relationships, as with the world around us, there are always dark nights that are followed by beautiful days.

Mother often said: "No one is perfect!" In love, as in other relationships, we must accept the flaws in others and hope that they will accept ours.

To expect your partner to be perfect, or to compete to see who can be best, is a childish game that no one wins. But when we work together on a personal or material project, for the betterment of either or both of us, then we both win in immeasurable ways.

14

Do You Take this Man...

At this writing it is apparent that, when it comes to the question of whether or not two adults of the same sex are allowed to marry, the laws of the United States are not united. The voters in most states have literally said: "not in my back yard, you don't!" In the mean time, the governing bodies of a few well meaning states have tried to appease the hundreds of thousands that plead for equal rights, by offering us "partnership agreements." In my view this is simply an attempt by those states to put into legalese, something that we can accomplish through our friendly local lawyer.

However, no matter in what state you might reside, unmarried couples, be they of the same sex or even senior citizens of opposite sex, are still not allowed the same automatic rights to inherit the partner's property, or for that matter, the right to visit a dying partner in some hospitals, or to make decisions for one's partner if he is incapacitated. Therefore it is extremely important that we prepare for any unavoidable events, and make the legal and written agreements as soon as we consider ourselves in a lifetime relationship. If you don't put these agreements in writing, you're skating on thin ice...and I hear the ice cracking as the two of you go dancing out across that frozen pond! Yes, spring is here, your love is blooming, and the ice is thawing. So stop procrastinating and get with it!

Mutual agreements in writing, about how assets such as real estate (your home), are purchased and paid for, should be signed by both parties and preferably notarized. Then, for the consideration of each of you, you need to come to full agreement in three serious areas. Face up to it, there is always a remote possibility of separation; and no one is spared the inevitability of sickness and death. Make your commitment *stronger than a marriage*, bite the bullet and *put it all in writing!*

Joint assets and bank accounts. If you purchase a home or any other real estate together, take the title as *joint tenants with right of survivorship*. Do the same with any joint bank accounts. With brokerage accounts and retirement accounts, contact the institution for the appropriate forms. And, see to it that they follow your instructions.

Health care and financial powers of attorney. Each person needs a copy of *one health care and one financial power of attorney*. These can be attained through an attorney or, if the situation isn't complicated, there are "do it yourself" kits and software.

Wills. Without a will the state decides who gets what. In that case blood relations would come first, and the partner may be left high and dry! When money is involved, believe me, relatives can soon forget what the deceased said (but didn't write). There are will kits and software available. However, if the estate is half a million or more, contact an attorney.

Disclaimer: I'm not an attorney, and I recommend that you see yours. However, I've had ample experience with both a divorce from a hetero marriage and now, over twenty years in a very strong gay partnership. Take my word for it…put it in writing and make it legal. After these matters are under your belt, the rest is heaven!

15

Making a Home

Whether you believe in heaven and hell, nirvana, the infinite, no here-after, or "take it as it comes," in this life there is just one person responsible for the finale, and that's you! Hopefully you're happy with your religion and/or philosophy and your final step-over will be peaceful and beautiful.

In the meantime, getting to know and respect yourself is the basis of a healthy relationship with the rest of the finite world.

In order for a dictatorship or any oppressive government to succeed, it must first rob us of our self-respect. Don't let anyone take that from you!

Second to self esteem is the value of a personal relationship with another human being. Some do not want to risk involvement in such relationships. They may fear disenchantment, a tragic separation or other division. These people may have been hurt before or they may feel a binding relationship would be too confining, or worse, too devastating to lose.

But nature has provided bonding and love for many very good reasons: There is the relationship of plants and of animals to each other, of domesticated animals to humans, of parents to children, children to one another, men to women and, of course...women to women and men to men. Along the way some of us decide to stop as singles and, feeling safe there, we may wish to remain. Then there are those who simply prefer a relationship with the out of doors, with Mother Nature.

In establishing a bond or relationship with another adult, we must "handle with care." This is not a simple matter of "How about a game of marbles?" Or "I'll feed this dog and care for him, so he'll love and obey me." And of course there are some who may wish to carry these games to unique extremes, like: "Let's play tennis and after the game I'll play you out in bed." Or "How about moving in with me? We'll dress in leather and you'll be my slave." Really? Whatever.

The decision to accept coupling must first be decided, that it's right for number one, with introspection and serious honesty. It makes no sense to ask someone else to commit himself to a relationship when you haven't thought it out yourself.

When you live alone you can stay comfortable in your lovely little cocoon. You might be able to avoid having your family and your non-gay associates know that you're gay. I know that some feel that their career, their family's attitudes and their general relationships outside of the gay community are too precious to risk one's own true exposure. But think about it. Are you always going to live your life in solitary confinement—in self imposed exile—constantly on guard, "protecting" others from the truth?

As I age (we all do, you know) and hopefully get a little wiser, I only wish that I could have made the decision to "live my own life" at an earlier age. Our submission to the social prejudices of the bigoted, at the cost of personal freedom and integrity, is as tragic for us as it has been for much of the international Jewish community, as well as it has been for other minority communities.

So, when in pursuit of Mr. Wonderful, don't deceive him and yourself by making this a senseless game of cat and mouse. Think ahead. The moment of truth will one day come upon you and you'll need to "fish or cut bait." If you do want the companionship but not the commitment, break it to him gently and be honest—let him know that, for the present, your career has to come first.

However, on the other hand, if you're ready, really be ready, then go for it! Because after you buy that condo together and both names are on the same mailbox, it's going to become obvious to friends and relatives as well, that you've become a pair of single men who have lived together for a few years now and "they must be gay!"

Living together, sharing an apartment or home is not simply a warm and fuzzy existence, it's very practical as well. You'll find you can afford to enjoy more in life, to have nicer things and to take better vacations, because you're sharing the costs.

After you've done a lot of talking together, you've learned that you're sexually compatible, discussed philosophy, politics, religion, etc., then that awesome time may have come to share a home.

I think I have pretty much the same feelings as most people, well, most *gay* people, and I don't want my life and emotions crushed after becoming deeply involved. So with the goal in mind of a blissful home, shared with the one you love, you should, in fact you must, ask serious probing questions before getting completely entangled.

This may all sound quite cold and calculated, and I know that sex and sentiment are exciting; But without serious thought and good sense, sex and sentimentality alone won't make for a long lasting relationship.

Your prospective house-mate may or may not be into writing things down. So it's up to you to at least do a written analysis of the situation. If he doesn't participate make it a point to bring these things up and see how he reacts. Remember, if this relationship is going to jell, you'll be spending a *lot* of time together. You want this to have a strong foundation and, if you're both very fortunate, there will never be a reason to lie.

Here's a list of questions to ask yourself, and then to ask him. Take what you want from the list…ask them all or just pick those you feel have not yet been answered. If you are afraid to ask certain questions before a binding relationship begins, it may be impossible to ask them (the answers may be too devastating) after you've both made this commitment. Heterosexual couples would also be better off if they did a good analysis before jumping into marriage. But, unlike gays, they have to rely on their government and churches for outside guidance and even legal support.

So, here we go:

1. What can *I* offer this relationship?
2. What can *he* offer this relationship?
3. What are *my* faults? (They'll probably always be with me.)
4. What are *his* faults? (Don't expect to change him.)
5. How do I believe this relationship will affect my life?
6. Will the emotional and sexual relationship hold up, and for how long?
7. If emotional and sexual attraction dwindles, can the relationship survive, and how?
8. If I had a previous relationship, why didn't it last?
9. Would this be the same for him and if not, why not?
10. Do I have to take the lead in a home-centered relationship?
11. How will we make decisions?
12. Are any expressions of our relationship acceptable in public and to what extent?
13. Away from career obligations, how much of our time can be spent together?
14. Will we want time away from each other such as with families or on separate vacations?
15. Will we want individual time for separate sports, walking, biking, or just meditation, and how much?

16. How will decisions be made about vacations, entertaining, activities and events?

17. How will conflicts be dealt with…avoided, discussed, fought out, negotiated?

18. Do either of us have a history or background of physical abuse?

19. How will our chores be divided in the home?

20. What chores do *I* dislike?

21. What chores does *he* dislike?

22. How important is the relative income of one partner to the other?

23. How are expenses and financial obligations to be divided and to be met?

24. Is this to be a monogamous relationship?

25. Is flirting with others acceptable and to what degree?

26. Do I have a medical or mental problem that he should understand?

27. Does he have a problem I should understand?

28. Do either, or both of us, consider adopting or assisting in the raising of a child or children and, if so, are we prepared for the long term responsibilities involved?

These are 28 subjects that are likely to arise in a gay relationship. Yes, any one of them can be an explosive issue…especially if it comes as an unpleasant surprise. That's why they're here, up-front. I firmly believe it is vital that both parties expect and accept change. *Nothing is as certain as change.* People, environments, careers, friends, the world…they're all in a constant state of change. After you've reviewed each of these questions and had a chance to discuss them with Mr. Wonderful…come to some agreements. These agreements aren't to be written in stone. Be prepared to re-negotiate and accept the possibility that he too may want to change along the way. Don't demand that he "go by the rules!" A great thing about really knowing who your mate is, is that you'll start sensing he wants change before it actually happens. Then you can give him the opening and offer to re-consider some previous understanding.

Along this line, don't deny anger until it explodes. Give your mate a sign, some warning, that you need space and time to think things out. And, after you've had a chance to cool down, if there is really a problem, face it and verbally get it out in the open. Pent-up feelings of anger can cause serious emotional problems and they can be the cause for lies, deceit and complete misunderstanding.

If a problem comes about, anger has been expressed and a solution doesn't seem to be forthcoming, ask for a chance to think. First, take some time to think of and to appreciate his good qualities. *Then* write out the problem and especially cover the underlying issues. Ask him to do the same. Maybe you need to sleep on it. After you've both cooled off, exchange your written analysis. Hopefully you can then discuss the problems in a rational manner. Here are some pointers when writing out problems (and be sure he has a look at these):

1. Write down a few of the things about him that you especially respect and love.

2. Then, be specific and brief about what the current problem is from your viewpoint.

3. Don't "dump" on your partner about problems he may have that you've both accepted.

4. Don't "keep the ball in his court." Acknowledge that this might be your problem, because of your viewpoint or idiosyncrasies.

5. Don't make general condemnations about what he does, or the way he relates to you.

6. Do ask for his understanding.

7. Be specific with your suggestions about the way you can cooperate to solve the problem.

Always be aware that your partner needs the same love and understanding as you need. Each and every one of us have the need to feel wanted and accepted.

It's sad to say that some have had to deny themselves the pleasure of a relationship. This is often an emotional wall that was built up for survival, due to harsh psychological conditions inflicted during childhood or even in adult life. Especially in the gay community we witness the outcome of cruel bigotry by others. So please, always consider the sensitive underlying feelings of your partner. As love overcomes these problems, you'll find the rewards are wonderful! Easy does it.

When it comes to pairing up, there is an alternative to "jumping in with both feet." It's an escape mechanism, that helps each of you retain your value as an individual.

Say that you both agree, you and your lover aren't ready for a binding relationship. Being brutally honest about it, you both agree that, though you've gotten involved, you haven't found that it's working out all that well.

Ideally, you can find a place with two bedrooms and two baths. Consider this sharing of a home first like a business partnership. Agree that all costs will be divided down the middle. Use the check-list and analyze how you might set up this relationship. You are simply sharing a home, you aren't in it as committed partners.

Maybe you are sexually compatible, so you can share his bedroom, or he yours, when you both feel the urge. You might even keep your private bedrooms and from time to time enjoy "dating" each other. If the relationship doesn't get or stay serious (maybe there are too many things you can't agree on) then simply stay friends, share expenses and retain your own parts of the house, but with unattached identities. It remains a real estate partnership (a Realtor, preferably gay or lesbian, can set it up that way) and you agree to keep it that way as long as that works out best for both of you. Who knows, maybe someday it can be more. Whether you're just sharing a home, or making it a life-long commitment, here are a few reminders:

- First remember that you're two gay males who have a tremendous amount in common …both physically and mentally…enjoy it!
- Avoid high powered flirting with others if he feels that he's the only one.
- Don't leave used condoms in plain view. No one likes to be told about your sex activities in that fashion.
- Don't rub his nose in how you've sacrificed for him. He's sacrificed too, and martyrdom does not make for a strong relationship.
- Never criticize or argue with him in front of others.
- On a date, don't wear leather when he's wearing slacks and vice versa.
- Never listen in on a phone extension unless invited.
- Brush your teeth in the A.M. and P.M. and/or use a mouthwash, especially before getting passionate.
- Don't lose his place in a book.
- Never announce his sexual eccentricities to others.
- His mail is private…don't trespass.
- Don't tell him why you hated your ex-lover or ex-wife; it may give him premonitions.

16

Listen to Your Mother

Mother always told me that I should set personal goals. She was right! I've found that it's important to one's self-worth and to one's participation in the human race that we achieve personal goals and have the satisfaction of a reasonable amount of attainments. We all need to feel the pleasure of accomplishment, especially in the fulfillment of loving and being loved. These are needs that motivate most human endeavors…they're a basic involvement in the family of man.

To get enjoyment from this life, and to give all that we can offer, we should find a profession or a plan for "plowing our precious earth and working the soil" in whatever way that is personally satisfying and pleasing. Don't let work become a chore. If you do, you aren't doing anyone a favor—least of all yourself!

As much as possible, be honest with others and let them know and love the *real you*. Deception is tragic. The greatest sin is to live your life under the rules of those who are prejudiced and those who are dominating egocentrics. Believe me, those people will never be satisfied!

Last, but by all means not least, express your love! Most of us were fortunate in having parents that, from birth, taught us love. If you have the capacity to love, no matter what else may have happened in your childhood, you should be grateful that your parents nurtured those feelings within you. Remember, those who say they can not love, those are the ones who need your compassion and empathy the most. Be considerate of others, and don't be afraid to express your positive feelings. I predict that the person who accepts your love, can and will give you his love in return.

"Does he love me? *Yes, he does!*"

About the Author

St. Charles was hatched, raised, and continues to make his nest, in Southern California. As an introverted kid of sixteen, his mother sent him to a Dale Carnegie Course to bring him out of his shell. It did; then he snuck *out* of the closet!

At twenty-one he was managing a resort hotel in Carmel Valley, California. He was drafted into the army and in the service he managed an officers' club, where he also wrote a weekly newspaper column in Fukuoka, Japan.

He has developed two corporations and, has overseen the training of hundreds of sales and management people in the hospitality and service industries. St. Charles established a foundation for east-west relations and he has received awards as a Buddhist Sunday School teacher. Certified as a Travel Counselor, he is also a Peer Counselor at a Gay & Lesbian Center.

Divorced after marriage and rearing a son; for over twenty years he has been in a gay partnership.

www.ingramcontent.com/pod-product-compliance
Lightning Source LLC
Chambersburg PA
CBHW031239280526
45784CB00004B/1637